THiS BOOK BELONGS TO

. . . .

FOR KIMWEI, SCOTT AND AARON, FOR
HELPING ME UNDERSTAND WHAT'S GOING
ON IN THE WORLD AND FOR HOLDING MY
HAND WHEN I GOT SAD ABOUT IT.

WORLD-
WHIZZING
FACTS

BLOOMSBURY CHILDREN'S BOOKS
Bloomsbury Publishing Plc
50 Bedford Square, London, WC1B 3DP, UK
29 Earlsfort Terrace, Dublin 2

BLOOMSBURY, BLOOMSBURY CHILDREN'S BOOKS and the Diana logo
are trademarks of Bloomsbury Publishing Plc

First published in Great Britain 2021 by Bloomsbury Publishing Plc

A catalogue record for this book is available from the British Library

ISBN: PB: 978-1-5266-0243-5; eBook: 978-1-5266-2357-7

2 4 6 8 10 9 7 5 3 1

Printed and bound in Great Britain by CPI Group (UK) Ltd, Croydon CR0 4YY

MIX
Paper from
responsible sources
FSC® C020471
FSC
www.fsc.org

To find out more about our authors and books visit
www.bloomsbury.com and sign up for our newsletters

DR EMILY GROSSMAN

WORLD-WHIZZING FACTS

ILLUSTRATED BY ALICE BOWSHER

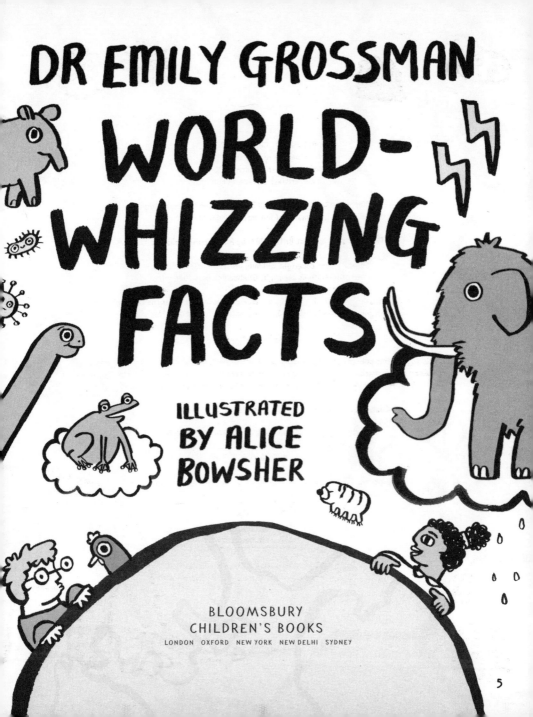

BLOOMSBURY
CHILDREN'S BOOKS

LONDON   OXFORD   NEW YORK   NEW DELHI   SYDNEY

CONTENTS

OUR WORLD is AMAZING!

Hi, I'm **Dr Emily.** You might remember me from my **Brain-fizzing Facts** book. In which case, **welcome back!** Or we might be meeting for the **first time** – in which case, **hello!**

Before we **start**, there's one **important** thing you need to **know** about me. I ask a **LOT** of **questions**. And I love **figuring stuff out** and **finding things out about** the **world**. My **favourite** feeling is when things **make sense**. That's what I love most about **science**. That **EVERYTHING** makes sense and that everything happens for a **reason**.

In this book I'll be **sharing** with you some of my **favourite things** about **our planet**, and explaining **WHY** they happen. But first I'll be asking YOU **questions** and asking you to try and **figure out** the answers for yourself. So give them a go. I'll always give you **four options** to choose from as the answer. If you don't **know** the right answer straight away, don't worry – **mistakes** make your **brain spark** and that's how you **learn**. Just start by **figuring out** if there are any answers that you know **CAN'T** be true, and **why**. And then see if you can think of a **sensible** reason why one of the others **MIGHT BE**. And you may well be **right**.

And remember, in science there's really no such thing as a **stupid question**. Or indeed a **wrong answer**. Truly. Wrong answers are just the **way** that we get to the **right one**.

Some of the facts in this book are totally **random**. They're **weird** things about the world that I've **discovered** or **read about** in my time as a **scientist**. Some might make you **laugh**. Some might **shock** you. And some are downright **gross**.

But **some** of them are about the things that **humans** have been doing to our **planet**, and about how our planet is **changing**. They are about how the Earth is **heating up** and how our planet's **land** and **natural resources** are being used up.

And about how lots of **animals, plants** and **humans** are **suffering** as a result.

These parts of the book might make you a bit **sad**. Or **scared**. Or **anxious**. Or **angry**. But don't worry, I'll be right there **with you** and I'll be giving you lots of **ideas** as we go along as to **small things** that you and your family can do to **help**. Plus, I'll be sharing lots of **inspiring stories** about **exciting things** that are going on in the world today that will give you **hope** and show you that the world can be a **better place**. If we all **work together** to make it so.

So, are you **ready** for the first question? Great. Then let's get **started**.

DR EMILY XX

WHICH WAY IS A DOG MORE LIKELY TO FACE WHILE WEEING?

A TOWARDS ITS OWNER

B TOWARDS ITS KENNEL

C TOWARDS ANOTHER DOG

D TOWARDS THE NORTH OR SOUTH POLE

It's a sunny Sunday morning and you stumble downstairs to find your favourite **canine companion** scratching away at the back door. You open it up ... and she **dashes** out into the back garden, chases a **squirrel** up a tree, and then **squats** down and does a **wee** ... right in the middle of the lawn. Pretty standard doggy behaviour.

But have you ever stopped to notice **which way** your furry friend usually **faces** when she is, err, **relieving herself?** I don't suppose you have. I mean, why on Earth would you?

Well, this is exactly what a **strange** team of scientists in Germany and the Czech Republic did. For **TWO YEARS.** That's quite a **commitment.**

The team monitored a group of **70 dogs** from **37 different breeds**. Every time one went for a **wee** or a **poo** (the dogs, not the scientists) they made a note as to which way the dog was standing. Well, probably not **EVERY** time. I'm sure they didn't get up in the night to **wee-watch**. But between them, the scientists recorded a **grand total** of **1,893 poos** and **5,582 wees**.

When the scientists compared notes, they noticed something rather **strange**. It seemed that the dogs were far more likely to do their business while **facing** either directly **north** or **south**. Weird or what?

THE **ANSWER** is **0**

A DOG IS MORE LIKELY TO FACE TOWARDS THE NORTH OR SOUTH POLE WHILE WEEING.

But why do dogs do this? Sounds **barking mad** to me.

Well, the truth is that no one really knows. But it would appear that dogs are pretty good at **sensing** the **Earth's magnetic field**. This is an **invisible force field** that radiates out from the Earth's **core** and **surrounds** the planet, giving rise to the **North and South Poles**. It's as if the Earth has one ginormous **bar magnet** running right through the middle of it.

Sailors use the Earth's magnetic field to work out **which way** they are going when they are **lost at sea**. You see, the **needle of a compass** will always **point** towards the **North Pole**. And by working out which way is **north**, and roughly where they are on a **map**, sailors can figure out which way to sail to get **home**.

It is thought that our **doggy friends** might have their own sort of **internal compass** that enables them to **sense** the Earth's magnetic field. How **cool** is that?

Dogs are not the **only** animals who are able to do this. Next time you come across **cows** grazing in a field, **deer** standing in a line or **ducks** landing on a lake, whip out your **compass** ... you might be rather **surprised** to discover that they will probably

be facing **directly** towards the **north** or **south**.

So, next time you're out for a walk and you **lose your way**, just wait for your doggy companion to **cock his leg**, and then follow his **nose**.

Speaking of **cocked legs**, did you know that it is usually only **male dogs** that raise their back leg in the air when they wee? They do this funny manoeuvre to **mark their territory**. The **higher** they manage to spray their yellow **calling-card** onto the nearest **tree** or **lamp-post**, the more likely it is that the **stinky scent** will be caught by the **wind** and travel **further away**, alerting nearby **canine competitors** to their presence.

Some animal experts think that dogs try to raise their leg as **high** as possible so they can **pretend** to the next sniffers who happen to pass by that they are **bigger** and **more intimidating** than they actually are. This might explain why you sometimes see a tiny little **sausage dog** doing a kind of **doggy handstand**, spraying his wee **all the way** up a lamp-post.

i MAY BE SMALL BUT i SURE CAN WEE!

Some **wild dogs** in Africa have taken this a step further. To appear as **big** as they can be, they try to **run up tree trunks WHILE** they are weeing! Maybe they hope that the next doggy visitor will think that there's a **ginormous tree-weeing beast** in the area and run for the hills in **terror**.

I wonder **how long** it would take this huge beast to do a wee? Ages, probably. Certainly **far longer** than it would take you or me to wee, right? Not **necessarily ...**

WHICH CREATURE WOULD TAKE THE LONGEST AMOUNT OF TIME TO WEE?

A AN ELEPHANT

B YOU

C A SMALL DOG

D THEY ALL TAKE THE SAME AMOUNT OF TIME

How long does it take you to do a wee when you've got a **full bladder?** You know, when you're **proper bursting**.

We can probably assume it would take you **longer** than it would take, say, a **small spaniel**. Right? I mean, the cute little thing only has a **tiny bladder's-worth of wee** to get rid of.

And surely we can assume that you'd take **less time** to wee than an **enormous elephant** with a **huge** bladder full of wee? Well, amazingly, we'd be **wrong** on **both** counts.

Scientists studied all sorts of weeing animals (lucky them) and discovered that most mammals that are bigger than a rabbit take the **same amount of time** to empty their bladders. A whopping **21 seconds!** That's a pretty **big wee**. Scientists were so excited to discover this **weird** fact that they even gave it a name. They called it, wait for it ... **THE UNIVERSAL LAW OF URINATION.**

TOILET

THE **ANSWER** is **D**
DOGS, HUMANS AND ELEPHANTS ALL TAKE THE SAME AMOUNT OF TIME TO WEE.

But **how** can this be? After all, all animals **squeeze** their wee out using the same amount of **pressure** from their bladder muscles. So surely the **time** it takes any mammal to wee should depend on how **big** it is, or at least how big its **bladder** is, and therefore **how much wee** there is to **let out?** Well, actually, it **doesn't**.

You see, here's the thing. In animals with **bigger bladders,** the **tube** leading from their bladder to the **outside world** (called the **urethra**) is also **wider**. This means that **more wee** can flow out of the bladder every second. Plus, in a wider tube, more of the wee can **flow freely** through the middle of the tube without having to **drag against the resistance** of its **inside edges,** so overall the wee flows **faster**. In the same way, a wide river flows **much faster** than a narrow stream, especially the water right in the **middle** of it.

WE ALL WEE TOGETHER!

Overall, this means that in bigger animals a much **larger VOLUME** of wee can **shoot out** of their **urethra** every second. We could say they have a **faster flow-rate**.

This faster flow-rate **balances out** the fact that the animal has a **bigger bladder** (and therefore a larger **volume** of wee to let out in the first place), meaning that overall a **huge hulking elephant** will take the **same amount of time** to empty its bladder as a **cute little spaniel**. This **balancing out** of flow-rate and bladder size explains why **ALL** mammals bigger than a **rabbit**, including **humans**, take the **same amount of time** to wee. No matter what **size** or **shape** they are.

Maybe, like me, you are now wondering about the **weeing habits** of mammals **smaller** than rabbits? Well, you see, cute little **fluffies** like rabbits and rats are so small that gravity doesn't allow them to wee out their urine in one long **flow** – their wee is more like a little spray of individual **droplets**, which is why they are not included in this particular **flow-based** fact.

Speaking of doing a wee, do you want to know something pretty **disgusting** about **toilets**? Thought so. Well, every time you **flush** the toilet, water droplets from the toilet bowl stay in the air for up to **2 hours** and can travel as far as **2 metres (m) from the toilet!**

That's about as far away as your **toothbrush** ... Yuck. I told you it was **disgusting**. But don't worry, your body is very **clever** and can kill most of the **bacteria** that try and get in by **trapping** them in sticky **mucus** in your airways, or **killing** them using the **acid** in your stomach. Phew. But if you're still **worried**, you can always **close the lid** before you flush.

Toilets may be pretty **revolting**, but how do **toilet seats** compare to some other less obviously **germ-filled** places you may end up putting your fingers?

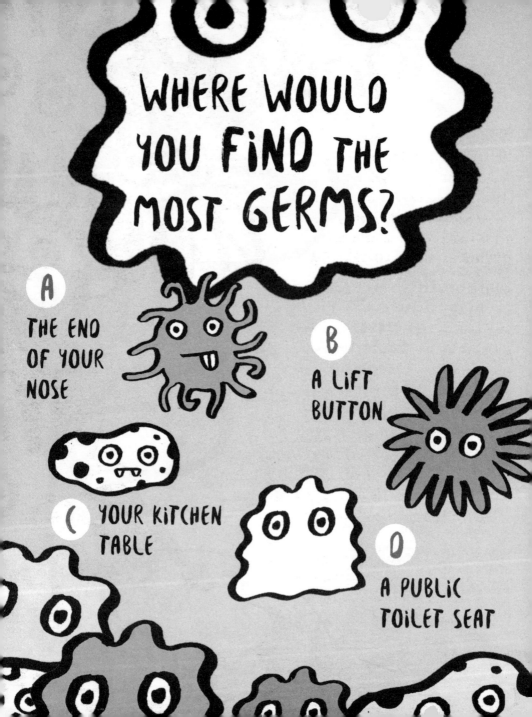

The end of your nose can get pretty **grubby**, right? Especially if you've been rolling about in the mud. But as long as you've had a **wash** recently, surely it can't be covered in as many **germs** as, say, a **toilet seat**?

Well, it all depends on what we mean by **germs**.

Often when people think of germs, they think of **bacteria**. And bacteria live **everywhere**. Bacteria are **teeny tiny** living creatures. They are sometimes known as **microorganisms** because they are **so small** that you can only see them using a **microscope**. In fact, around **1,000** of the little critters would fit onto the tip of just one of the **hairs on your head!**

You can find bacteria in the air, in water, in the soil and on most **surfaces** ... and especially in and around **living creatures**.

Take a look at your **hands.** They probably look pretty **clean,** right? Just some plain old hands, not much to see there, other than your **skin.** Unless of course you've been eating some **sticky toffee pudding** with your fingers.

YUM.

But even if you haven't, you might be surprised to know that, **right now,** your hands (and mine) are likely to be home to more than **3,000 individual bacteria** from about **150 different species.** In fact, you have your own **unique** set of hand-bacteria, called your **bacterial fingerprint.** You see, not only does your body have lots of its **own** bacteria, but your hands are also always **touching** things and picking up **new** bacteria from **all over the place.** And anywhere your **hands** go ... the bacteria go too. Like onto the **pages** of this **book.** Or a **biscuit tin.** Or the end of your **nose.**

This means that **anything** that is regularly **prodded** or **touched** or **picked up** by lots of different people is likely to be **even more** covered in bacteria than your own hands – especially if it's one of those things that people don't tend to consider **cleaning** very often. Like your TV **remote control**. Or a shop **door handle**. Or the **keyboard** of your classroom **computer**.

A place that's touched by an **AWFUL LOT** of **different** fingers is ... you guessed it ... a **lift button**. People are constantly **pressing** lift buttons, and **WHO KNOWS** where all those **grubby** fingers have been?

Indeed, when scientists analysed **samples** from a variety of lift buttons in hospitals, restaurants, banks, offices and airports, they found that a typical **lift button** has nearly 40 times more bacteria on it than a **public toilet seat**. EWWWW.

So, a lift button is the **clear winner**, right? Not so fast ...

If we were talking about places with the **most bacteria** on them, then yes, a lift button would win **hands down**. But here's the thing: we were **supposed** to be figuring out the place with the most **GERMS**. And, contrary to popular belief, **not all bacteria are germs**.

So, before you panic and try to **scrub off** all the bacteria from your hands after taking the lift, let me **reassure** you that the **majority** of bacteria found in and around your **body** (and therefore on lift buttons) are actually perfectly **harmless**. In fact, they can often be rather helpful.

Without the **friendly bacteria** living in your **gut**, for example, you wouldn't be able to **digest** your food properly or **fight off diseases**. In fact, there are around **three times** more **good bacteria** in your body than there are **body cells**. That's a bonkers **100 trillion** or so helpful little creatures living happily **inside** you. If you **clumped** them all together, they'd form a lump the size of a **football**, weighing more than your **brain!**

Bacteria are not just useful to **living** creatures. Some are pretty good at **breaking down** dead and decaying plant and animal matter. This helps to return **useful nutrients** to the **soil**, such as nitrates that are needed for **plants** to grow.

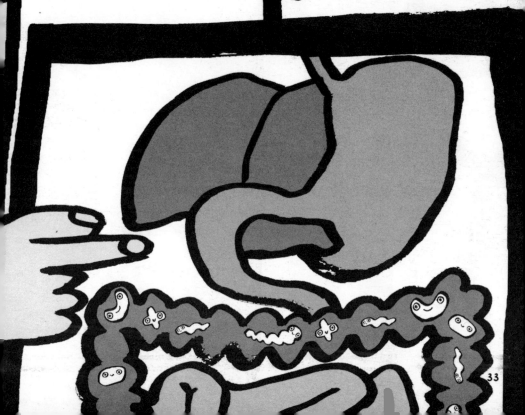

33

AH-AH -AH- CHOOOO!

However, not **ALL** bacteria are helpful. In fact, some can be a right old **nuisance**, causing infections, sore throats, tummy upsets, or diseases such as tuberculosis or cholera. These types of **disease-causing** bacteria – along with other nasty things like **viruses** and some types of **fungi** – are properly known as **pathogens**.

Pathogens can be found in the **saliva** or **snot** of people who have coughs, colds or other **infectious diseases**, as well as in **poo**, in raw meat and inside **dead things** as they start to **decay**. That's why it's really important to **wash your hands** after going to the **toilet**, blowing your **nose** or handling **raw meat**, and to **cover your mouth** when you cough or sneeze.

Now, here's the important part ...
It's these **PATHOGENS**, not just
any old bacteria, that are commonly
known as **germs.**

This brings us back to the original
question: where would you find the
most **germs?** In other
words, which places are
the most covered
in **HARMFUL**
bacteria?

VIRUSES ARE TINY
PARTICLES (MUCH SMALLER
THAN BACTERIA) THAT ARE MADE
UP OF GENETIC MATERIAL AND
PROTEINS. THEY CAN ONLY REPRODUCE BY
GETTING INSIDE THE CELLS OF OTHER
CREATURES. BECAUSE OF THIS, SOME
SCIENTISTS DON'T EVEN CONSIDER
VIRUSES TO BE ALIVE.

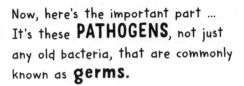

As we've discussed, most of the bacteria on your **hands** or on places you've been **touching** – such as the end of your **nose** or a **lift button** – are probably pretty harmless. Unless of course you've got a **stinking cold** and you've been wiping **snot** over it. Or **licking** it. Not that you **CAN** lick your **nose**. Or at least I can't. Can **you**?

This means that, whilst **lift buttons, noses** and other frequently-touched places may be covered in bacteria, they're not actually very **germy**.

OK, so what about your **kitchen table?** Well, it's likely to be covered in **friendly bacteria** because lots of people **touch** it. But there's also the **possibility** that someone has left some of last week's dinner **rotting away** on

FEWER THAN 1 IN EVERY 100 BACTERIA CAUSE DISEASES IN HUMANS.

a corner of it. Or chopped up some **raw chicken** without cleaning up properly afterwards. (Please don't do that.) Or allowed the cat to **do its business** slap bang in the middle of it. (Please don't do that either, that's just disgusting.) Therefore, a kitchen table, or indeed **ANY** kitchen **surface**, is a potential source of **germs** that could make you **sick**. That's why it's important to give the table a good **wipe down** with some **disinfectant** to kill any harmful bacteria before you **eat your dinner off it.** Not that you would. Especially if it's **soup**. That would just be silly. And rather **messy**.

KITCHEN TABLES CAN BE PRETTY GERMY THEN, BUT WHAT ABOUT TOILET SEATS?

Seeing as a toilet seat is the place where you plonk your **backside** when **relieving yourself**, it would make sense that it would be the place with the **most germs**. Not your backside, that's probably reasonably clean – assuming you've had a bath recently – but the **seat** where you sit to **expel** stuff from your **nether regions** might be more than a **wee bit yucky**. I mean, **toilet accidents** happen, right? And that's when lots of germs might get **sprayed** all over the seat.

Even though most toilet seats do get **cleaned** pretty regularly, the **bottom line** is that there's a good chance that, of all the suggested answers to this question, **toilet seats** would have the greatest number of **nasty germs** lurking on them.

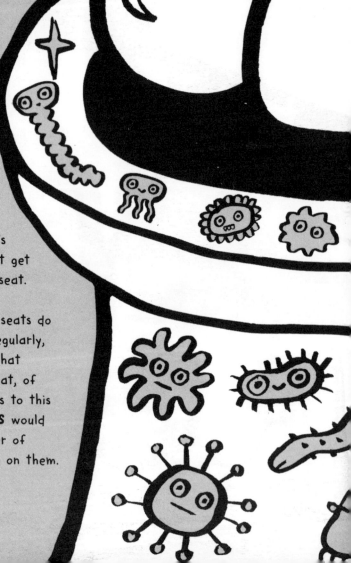

To answer this **disgusting-sounding** question, we need to understand a bit about **the water cycle**. All the water on our planet is part of what's known as a **closed system**, which means that the **same water** has been going around and around the same cycle for **millions of years**.

So how does this cycle **work?**

Let's begin with the water in the **oceans**. Heat from the Sun **warms the ocean surface**, causing **liquid** water molecules to gain **heat energy** and **jiggle about** a lot. Some of the molecules get **enough jiggle energy** (known as **kinetic energy**) that they **break free** from one another, leaving the surface of the ocean to form invisible **water vapour** – a **gas**. This process is known as **evaporation**.

Warm air above the oceans contains **lots** of this invisible water vapour, because the Sun's energy has **evaporated** lots of water from the **ocean surface**.

Warm air is **less dense** than the cool air above it, so it **rises** high up into the atmosphere to where it is **colder**, taking the **water vapour** with it. Higher up in the atmosphere, the **air pressure** is **lower**. This decrease in **pressure** allows the warm air to **expand**, so the molecules of water vapour **move apart** from each other and **spread out**. As they do this, they **lose** some of their **jiggle energy** and **cool down again**. If the molecules of water vapour get cool enough, they **are drawn back together again** to form **tiny droplets** of liquid water. These droplets hang around in the air, forming a **fine mist** that we call a **cloud**.

41

Once formed, clouds get **blown** across the sky by the **wind** until they reach an area where the air is **cooler.** Here, the molecules in the tiny water droplets lose **even more** of their jiggle energy, and this allows the droplets to come together to form **bigger droplets.**

When these droplets are **big and heavy enough,** they eventually **fall** from the sky as **rain.**

Sometimes **strong winds** can cause **storm clouds** to form. And sometimes when it's **REALLY COLD** the tiny water droplets in the clouds freeze into tiny ice crystals. The ice crystals stick together to make beautiful snowflakes that eventually fall as snow.

MILLIONS OF CLOUD DROPLETS ARE NEEDED TO FORM JUST ONE RAINDROP!

So what happens when the atmosphere becomes **WARMER?** Well, firstly, in areas of the world that are **already quite dry** (where there's **not much water vapour** hanging around in the air), the **extra heat energy** in the atmosphere will make it **even harder** for any water vapour in the air to **cool down enough** to condense and form **clouds**.

Fewer clouds means **less rain**, which xcan cause the land in these areas to **dry out** and **plants to die**, increasing the chances of **droughts, forest fires** and water **shortages**.

Warmer air in the atmosphere will also cause the oceans to become warmer, so there will be more evaporation. This means that more water vapour will end up in the air. Plus, warm air can actually HOLD more water vapour than cooler air. Overall, this means that when the atmosphere is warmer, there will be LOTS MORE WATER VAPOUR in the air. When all this extra water vapour is carried to areas of the sky where it is cool enough for clouds to form, there will not only be more clouds than usual, but the clouds will also be bigger and denser.

This means that in parts of the world that are already wet, there will be more frequent and heavier rainfall, as well as more extreme storms – leading to increased chances of flooding and damage to people's homes.

In countries where the air is **already very humid** (meaning there's **LOTS** of water vapour already **hanging around** in the air) – like in the **tropics** – the further **increase** in water vapour in the air can result in **more intense tropical storms, cyclones** and **monsoons**.

This combination of **dryer areas getting dryer** and **wetter areas getting wetter** – with more extreme weather events – is exactly the type of **climate change** that we are seeing across the globe today due to **global warming**. (I'll come back to this later.)

OK, so what has all this got to do with **weeing?** Well let's get back to the **water cycle.**

When **rain** hits the Earth, it seeps **deep** into the ground, eventually finding its way into **streams** and **rivers**. The rivers flow back into the **oceans** ... and the whole cycle starts **all over again** – around and around **forever.**

Now at some point during this cycle, pretty much **all creatures** will **take up** some of this water into their **bodies. Plants** do this by **absorbing** water from the **soil** through their **roots**, while most **animals** do this by **drinking.** (Shout-out to **frogs,** who absorb water through their **skin.**)

Plants **release** their water back into the **atmosphere** through a process called **transpiration,** in which water moves up through their **stem** and **evaporates** from their leaves. Animals, on the other hand, **keep hold** of the water they **need** and **excrete** the rest of it, along with **waste products** from the body, in the form of wee (properly known as **urine**). Animals also **lose** some water by sweating, breathing, crying ... and, yes, in their snot, vomit and poo.

Whether you're a **sophisticated** human being with access to a **toilet** or a stinky **pig** on a **farmyard**, your wee and sweat will eventually end up back in the ground and rivers – maybe via a **sewage plant**, where it is **filtered** and all the **nasty wee-chemicals** are removed, or via rocks and soil that act as **natural filtration systems**.

Either way, by the time the **watery** part has **evaporated** again to form **clouds**, the **impurities** will have been **left behind** and only **pure water** will re-join the **water cycle**. This means that the water cycle will always contain **some water** that was once sitting in the **bladder** of a pig. Or your **best friend.** Or your **teacher.**

NOT SO FAST ...

SO, I GUESS THAT MEANS THE ANSWER TO THIS QUESTION MUST BE PIG WEE AND HUMAN WEE, RIGHT?

In lots of countries (including the UK, the US and much of Europe), water is **collected** from rivers, reservoirs, or underground water stores known as **aquifers** – or directly from our **toilet sewage** – and sent to **water treatment centres** to be **cleaned**. The clean water is then stored in **massive tanks** that are connected to the **mains water supply pipes**. These pipes bring clean water all the way to the **roads** near your house. The water flows through **smaller pipes** right into your **home**, then runs out of your **kitchen tap** and straight into your **glass**.

Unless of course you buy **bottled** water, which **supposedly** comes directly from a **mountain stream**. While bottled water is **extremely important** for many people across the globe, if you live in a country where your tap water has been **cleaned** and is therefore **safe to drink**, I wouldn't **bother** if I were you.

FOR SALE

Bottled water is the same **boring old** water as drinkable tap water; it's just been **collected** from a **different place.** And sometimes even **THAT'S** not **true.** Shockingly, **more than half** of all bottled water actually comes from ... **the tap.** What a **rip-off!** And even if you happen to buy some that **doesn't,** studies show that when people are **blind-folded** they can't actually **taste** the difference.

So, unless you live somewhere where the tap water **isn't safe to drink,** don't **waste your**

money buying bottled water. Plus, as you probably know, plastic is not **biodegradable,** which means that it can't be **broken down.** Therefore, your plastic water bottle may well end up becoming part of the terrifying **300 kilograms (kg)** of **plastic pollution** that enters the **oceans EVERY SECOND,** causing untold damage to **fish** and other sea **creatures.**

Unfortunately, **recycling** isn't necessarily the answer to this problem. Shockingly, a huge proportion of 'recycled' plastic actually ends up in the **oceans** or sitting in **landfill** sites. There are now even large areas in the ocean where, due to ocean currents, enormous amounts of plastic **collect** in one place, resulting in **'garbage dumps of the sea'.**

It's definitely still a good idea to **separate out** any **recyclable** items from the rest of your rubbish, but the **BEST** idea is to **reduce** the amount of plastic that you use **in the first place.**

THE GREAT PACIFIC GARBAGE PATCH, WHICH IS HALFWAY BETWEEN HAWAII AND CALIFORNIA, CONTAINS MORE THAN 18,000,000,000,000 (18 TRILLION) PIECES OF PLASTIC, WEIGHS MORE THAN 43,000 CARS AND IS 3 TIMES THE SIZE OF FRANCE.

Anyway, where were we? Ah yes. The **point** is that **wherever** you fill your glass from, the water you drink will have come from **the water cycle.**

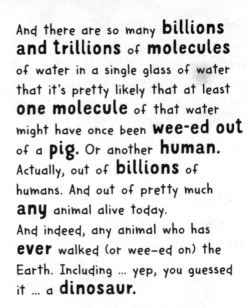

And there are so many **billions and trillions of molecules** of water in a single glass of water that it's pretty likely that at least **one molecule** of that water might have once been **wee-ed out** of a **pig**. Or another **human**. Actually, out of **billions** of humans. And out of pretty much **any** animal alive today.

And indeed, any animal who has **ever** walked (or wee-ed on) the Earth. Including ... yep, you guessed it ... a **dinosaur**.

THE **ANSWER** is **0**
EVERY TIME YOU TAKE A SIP OF WATER, IT'S PRETTY LIKELY THAT YOU'RE DRINKING PIG WEE, HUMAN WEE, DINOSAUR WEE AND INDEED ALL OTHER TYPES OF WEE!

Talking of the water cycle, clouds are all **light and fluffy,** right? Well, they might look like that, but have you ever **thought about** how much a cloud might actually **weigh?**

A cloud looks all **soft and squishy,** right? Kinda like a **giant marshmallow.** You might even imagine **snuggling up** on one and falling **fast asleep,** while angels play **pretty music** around your head. However, clouds aren't as **light and fluffy** as as they look.

You see, clouds are not just **empty space.** As we saw in the last chapter, clouds actually contain lots of tiny **water droplets.** And water droplets can be **HEAVY.** At least, they can be when there's **enough** of them.

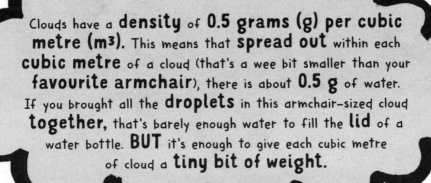

Clouds have a **density** of **0.5 grams (g) per cubic metre (m³).** This means that **spread out** within each **cubic metre** of a cloud (that's a wee bit smaller than your **favourite armchair**), there is about **0.5 g** of water. If you brought all the **droplets** in this armchair-sized cloud **together,** that's barely enough water to fill the **lid** of a water bottle. **BUT** it's enough to give each cubic metre of cloud a **tiny bit of weight.**

So how **big** is a cloud? The average **bit of fluff** up there in **cloud-land** may **LOOK** as small as a **ball of cotton wool**, but it is actually a **gigantic 1 cubic kilometre (km³)** in size. That's the length of about 10 football pitches. **IN EACH DIRECTION!**

A **cubic kilometre** is pretty darn big. You probably know that **1 kilometre (km)**, which is a measure of length, contains **1,000 metres (m)**. So, **1 km³**, which is a measure of **volume**, contains ...

1000 m x 1000 m x 1000 m = 1,000,000,000 m³

= **1 billion m³**

We know that **1 m³** of cloud contains around **0.5 g** of water droplets. This means that an average **1 km³** cloud will contain a **whopping great ...**

0.5 g per cubic metre x 1,000,000,000 m³ = **500, 000, 000 g** of water ...

Which in **kg** is ...

500,000,000 g ÷ 1000 = **500,000 kg** of water.

That's an **awful lot** of water in one cloud. No wonder a cloud would hurt you if it fell on your **head**. Even a large male African **elephant** only weighs about **6,000 kg**, so an **average cloud** would weigh the **same** as ...

500,000 kg ÷ 6000 kg = **83.3** African elephants.

Not that you **can have** 0.3 of an elephant. That would be a bit **weird**. Maybe we would call it an **ele**. Or maybe we should just say that it's **about 83** elephants.

THE **ANSWER** is **0** THE AVERAGE CLOUD WEIGHS ABOUT THE SAME AS 83 AFRICAN ELEPHANTS.

Speaking of **elephants**, did you know that an elephant's **poo** can be used for something rather **unexpected**?

Did you know that the average elephant spends **16–18 hours** a day **eating?** Imagine how **boring** that would be. Having to eat **ALL THE TIME.** When would you find time to **do your homework?** Or **build spaceships?**

Elephants are what's known as **herbivores,** which means that they only eat **plants.** Their **diet** consists mainly of grass, small plants, bushes, fruit, twigs and roots. Sometimes they also use their **sharp tusks** to **churn up** and eat **soil,** which contains useful **salt** and **minerals,** and to tear off strips of bark from **tree trunks.** Tree bark may not **seem** a very **appealing meal,** but it contains **calcium,** which strengthens the elephant's **bones,** and **roughage,** which helps their **digestive system.**

On an **average day,** an elephant will munch its way through a mighty **150–170 kg** of **vegetation.** To help them get through so much **woody** food, like all herbivores they have **special teeth** that are **adapted** to **grind up** plant tissue – a bit like your **molars** that help you to grind up **vegetables,** but much **harder** and with rough **ridges.** Even so, elephants' food is so **tough** and **fibrous** that **more than half** of what they eat passes straight through their body **undigested.** Yep, they **poo** it straight out. The average adult African elephant produces up to **140 kg of poo** every day. That's as heavy as a **small male gorilla.** Imagine **pooping** one of those out.

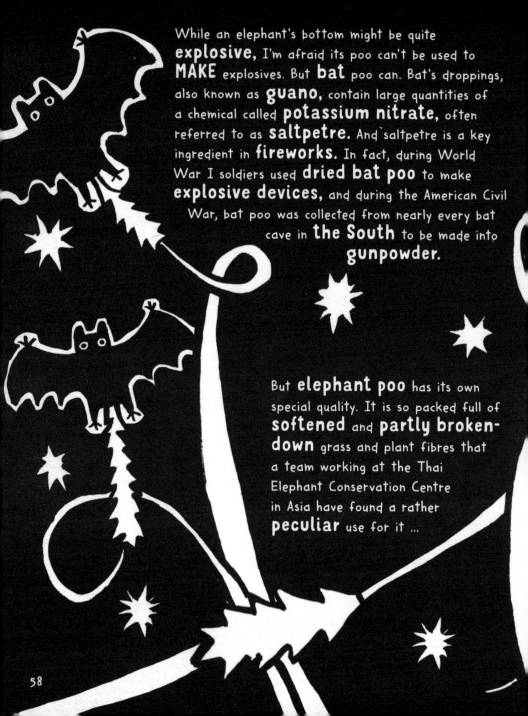

While an elephant's bottom might be quite **explosive,** I'm afraid its poo can't be used to **MAKE** explosives. But **bat** poo can. Bat's droppings, also known as **guano,** contain large quantities of a chemical called **potassium nitrate,** often referred to as **saltpetre.** And saltpetre is a key ingredient in **fireworks.** In fact, during World War I soldiers used **dried bat poo** to make **explosive devices,** and during the American Civil War, bat poo was collected from nearly every bat cave in **the South** to be made into **gunpowder.**

But **elephant poo** has its own special quality. It is so packed full of **softened** and **partly broken-down** grass and plant fibres that a team working at the Thai Elephant Conservation Centre in Asia have found a rather **peculiar** use for it ...

First, the giant lumps of poo are **washed** to separate out any **undigested hay**. Then the poo is **sterilised** to get rid of any **nasty bacteria**. It is then **blended** into a **fibrous pulp**, which is **spread** out into **large sheets** and left to **dry**. Once they're dry, the sheets are **cut** ... to make **paper!**

A single elephant can generate enough poo in one day to make over **100 pages of paper**, and at the Conservation Centre these **poo-pages** are turned into **homemade notebooks**.

THE **ANSWER** is **A** AN **ELEPHANT'S** POO CAN BE USED FOR MAKING NOTEBOOKS.

Using elephant poo to make books, photo-frames and posters has really **caught on** in conservation centres and safari parks across the globe. In fact, in Kenya there are now at least 17 **commercial firms** involved in making **high-quality paper** from an elephant's **stinky excretions**.

It's not just an elephant's **POO** that can be **useful** to humans ... Due to their **fibrous** eating habits, elephants can act as **'forest gardeners'** – trimming back **small shrubs** so that larger, **slow-growing trees** have a better chance of **survival.** These larger trees take in huge quantities of **carbon dioxide** from the air, storing the **carbon** in their leaves and **trunk.** (The tree's trunk, not the elephant's.)

Elephants' abilities to help the growth of **carbon-storing trees** means that they play an important role in **protecting** our planet from the damaging effects of **climate change.** This is why it's so important that we **look after** these **majestic** creatures, along with all the other **living beings** on our planet. I'll come back to this a bit later.

Sadly though, studies tell us that the number of **forest elephants** in Africa is **falling,** due, at least in **part,** to **poaching** and the **destruction** of their **habitats** (the places where they **live**). In fact, scientists **warn** that – due to a combination of **habitat destruction, overconsumption** (humans using up too much of the Earth's limited **resources**), **climate change** and **pollution** – around **a quarter** of **ALL** mammals may soon face **extinction.** I'll come back to this later too.

But for now, speaking of pollution, what about this **silly** idea that elephant poo might be capable of **cleaning dirty water?** Surely that must have been a **nonsense** suggestion? After all, animal waste is **CAUSING** huge **problems** in **waterways** across the globe. Let's quickly delve into that ...

Animal poo contains **nutrients**. As do the **chemical fertilisers** often used by farmers to grow **crops** to feed their animals. When it rains, animal poo and farmland chemicals **wash off the land** and into streams, rivers and lakes. Not only can this cause **contamination** of the water, but all the **extra nutrients** can lead to **extreme growth** of **green algae** in the water. The algae **grow and grow** until they eventually **cover the entire surface** of the water, **blocking light** from reaching **other plants** below the surface. Without light, these plants can't carry out **photosynthesis**, so they **die. Bacteria** then **feed off** the **dead plants**, using up the **oxygen** in the water that **fish** and other freshwater creatures **depend on**, which means these creatures are likely to **die too**.

This worrying process is known as **eutrophication**, and it is causing widespread problems **across the globe**. Problems that are being made **far worse** by the ever-increasing amount of **waste** produced by farm animals that are bred for **milk** or **meat**, and the increased use of **intensive farming practices** (ways of producing large amounts of crops using chemicals and machines) that require lots of **chemical fertilisers**. More on this later.

But back to **the point.** While animal poo can certainly **CAUSE** enormous **damage** to fresh water, it can also be used to **COMBAT** some forms of **water pollution.** In Bolivia, for example, **llama poo** is used to treat **poisonous water** leaking into the ground from **abandoned tin and silver mines.** Not only is this water **highly acidic,** but it also contains **toxic metals** that damage the local environment and can enter the

water **supplies** of nearby cities. However, **bacteria** living in llama poo (or probably any other type of poo, including that of an elephant) can **neutralise the acid** in the polluted water and can even remove some of the **dissolved metals.** Clever, eh?

Given that **300–400 million tonnes (t)** of heavy metals, solvents, toxic sludge and other wastes from industrial facilities are being **dumped** into the world's waters every year, it's possible that, in the future, **animal poo** may be of **vital use** to us. We just need to put the **right type** (and amount) of poo in the **right places.**

Luckily, there's no **shortage** of animal poo on the planet. Most creatures poo at least **once a day.** But did you know that there's an animal that only lets out its load **once a week?**

B A SLOTH

A A CAMEL

WHICH ANIMAL ONLY POOS ONCE A WEEK?

C A JELLYFISH

D A TARDIGRADE

Everyone needs to **poo**. Well, maybe not **right this second**, but at **some point**, we all need to **plop** one out. Whether you're a **pig** or a **penguin**, a **giraffe** or a **goldfish**, pooing is an essential way of getting rid of **waste substances** and **toxic chemicals** from your body.

Waste substances are produced by the body as a result of **eating food** – something all living creatures need to do in order to survive. OK **smarty pants**, except for **other plants** and some types of **algae**, which **make their OWN food** using **carbon dioxide** from the **air**, **water** from the **soil** (or the watery areas they grow in) and **energy** from **sunlight** – a process known as **photosynthesis**. Either way, whether they **eat** it or make **their own**, all living creatures require **food** because food releases **energy**. And energy is needed to **do fun things**, such as grow, move around, climb trees, make babies, keep warm at night or play the guitar.

WE MAKE OUR OWN FOOD!

So how does the process of **waste production** actually work? When you (or most other animals) **eat food,** your food first passes into your **stomach.** Here, the food mixes with **acid** to kill any nasty **bacteria,** and it begins to get broken down by **digestive enzymes** – small **chemicals** that help break down **big** food molecules (such as carbohydrates, fats and proteins) into **smaller** **ones.** The **partly digested** food then continues on into your **small intestine** (or **gut**). Here, more digestive enzymes are **released,** and the food molecules are broken down further. The breakdown of **fats** is helped by the addition of a chemical called **bile** that is produced by your **liver.** Bile also contains **old red blood cells** that your body needs to get rid of, which are what make your poo an **orangey-brown** colour.

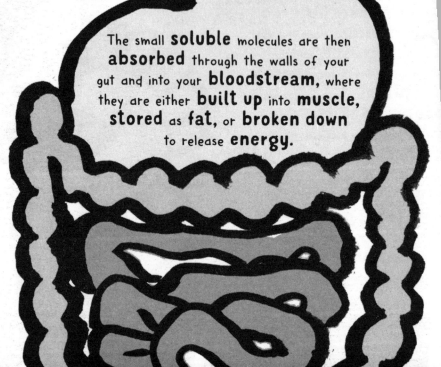

The small **soluble** molecules are then **absorbed** through the walls of your gut and into your **bloodstream,** where they are either **built up** into **muscle, stored** as **fat,** or **broken down** to release **energy.**

But here's the **important** bit. Any awkward **remnants** of food that can't be **broken down** or **absorbed** (such as indigestible **fibre**) – along with the bile and digestive juices – then pass into your **large intestine** as a **mushy brown sludge**. As this passes through the inside of your large intestine, **valuable water** (that was originally in your **food** or your **digestive** juices) gets **reabsorbed** through the walls of your intestine and **back into your body**, so the **sludgy brown** waste gets gradually **harder**. The waste continues to **move along** your large intestine until it eventually finds its way into your **rectum**. Here the waste is **stored** until you, or the animal, is ready to **excrete** it from its **anus** as **poo**.

That is, except for those few **unfortunate** creatures who **don't have an anus**. Like **jellyfish**. These slimy creatures excrete their waste out of the **same hole** that they take their **food** in through. Nice.

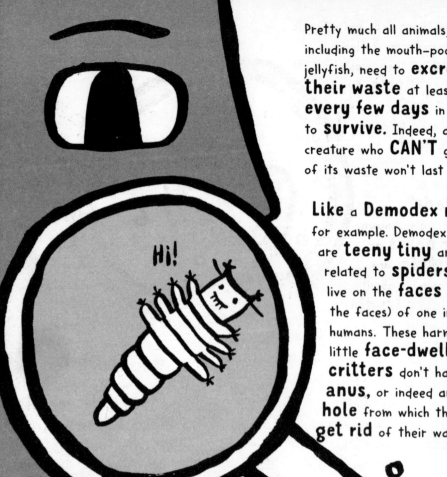

Pretty much all animals, including the mouth-pooping jellyfish, need to **excrete their waste** at least **every few days** in order to **survive**. Indeed, any creature who **CAN'T** get rid of its waste won't last **long**.

Like a **Demodex mite**, for example. Demodex mites are **teeny tiny** animals related to **spiders** that live on the **faces** (yes, the faces) of one in four humans. These harmless little **face-dwelling critters** don't have an **anus**, or indeed any other **hole** from which they can **get rid** of their waste.

Hi!

Instead, they just **store their waste** inside special large cells in their **abdomens** which get **bigger and bigger** ... until the poor little mites just **die**. Which usually happens after only a couple of weeks.

Other than these poor unfortunate souls, all animals must find ways to **get rid** of their waste **pretty regularly.** So, which **strange** creatures might only need to poo **once a week?**

What about a **tardigrade?**
Tardigrades, also known as **water bears** or **moss piglets,** are tiny little animals about **1 millimetre (mm)** long, with plump bodies and cute little **scrunched up** heads. They may look sweet, but they are the most **indestructible** creatures on Earth, able to **survive** at temperatures and pressures that would **destroy** every other type of organism. They can even survive in **outer space.**

Cute little tardigrades **moult** regularly, between **4–12 times** throughout their **3–30 months** of life. When they moult, they get rid of their **tough outer layer,** called their **cuticle,** along with their **claws** and some of the **lining of their gut.** Some types of tardigrade can **only get rid of their waste** during this **moulting process.** When these types of tardigrade moult, their **poo** becomes **detached from their body,** along with their **cuticle.** But while **some** tardigrades do excrete their waste in this very **unusual** way, which might only occur **once a month** or less, many other types of tardigrade **poo pretty regularly.**

So if it's not the Demodex mite, the jellyfish or the tardigrade, might our **weekly pooer** be a creature that poos so **rarely** because it has to **keep tight hold** of some of the more **useful** components of its poo, such as **water?**

Camels, for example, live in really **dry** areas, which means they certainly need to **hang onto** as much **water** as possible, which is why they store it in their **hump,** right?

Not so fast. Contrary to popular belief, camels' humps **DON'T** actually contain **water,** but are instead full of **fat.** Animals usually store fat **all over** their bodies, both to keep themselves **warm** and so they can convert it to **energy** when they need it. But because camels can store pretty much all the energy-giving fat they might need in their **hump,** they can afford to keep the **REST** of their body pretty much **fat-free.**

Without an **insulating layer** of **fat,** they are able to **lose heat** much more easily and **stay cool.**

Anyway, without a hump to store it in, a camel **hangs onto** as much **water** as possible by making its **wee** really **thick** – it has the consistency of **syrup.** And as for its **poo** ... well, the camel's large intestine **reabsorbs** as much water as possible from its **sludgy waste** back into its body.

However, this doesn't mean that camels poo **less often** than other animals, just that their poo comes out **really really dry.** So, our **skinny-legged** friend is not the answer.

Perhaps a creature that only poos once a week would be one that **digests** its food very **slowly,** so it rarely has **enough waste** to be worth **getting rid of?**

When it comes to doing things **slowly**, nothing beats the mighty **sloth**. Indeed, a **sluggish sloth** has such a **slow digestive system** that it can take a **whole month** for it to digest **a single leaf**. This means that the poor sloth barely gets **any energy**. No wonder it has to do everything at a **snail's pace**.

The result of a sloth's **super-slow digestion** is that its **food** moves through its digestive tract **extremely slowly**. So slowly, that the sloth only needs to **get rid** of the **waste** from its food about ... **once a week**. On this special **poo-day**, the sloth squeezes out a shocking **one-third** of its own body weight. This **gigantic poo-sausage** emerges in **one long piece** that is the size, shape and colour of a **rotten banana**.

But that's not the **weirdest** part. Rather than releasing its single **mega-poo** from the top of the **tree canopy** like other tree-living creatures, the sloth **descends** from its safe place up in the trees ... wait for it ... and poos at the **BASE** of its tree. And always in **exactly the same place**.

Old slothy climbs **very slowly** down to the ground, does a strange **poo-dance** as it digs itself a **hole**,

THE **ANSWER** is **B**
A SLOTH ONLY POOS ONCE A WEEK.

lets out its **dirty business** and then does another **little dance** to slightly **cover it up.** When the performance is over, it **slowly crawls** its way back up its tree to **safety.**

Not only does this **excruciatingly slow poo-process** take an **enormous** amount of the sloth's **time** and precious **energy,** it also **exposes** the poor sloth to **dangerous forest-floor predators.** The **slow-coach sloth** can't exactly just **run away** if one approaches. Indeed, around **half** of all sloths **die** when they are **down from their trees** – most probably when they're going to the **toilet.** What an **embarrassing** way to go ...

So **WHY** would a sloth **risk its life** every single week by coming down from its tree to poo, rather than just **scattering** their bottom-excretions from the **treetops?** The truth is, no one really knows. But some **experts** think that it is so that sloths can more precisely **mark their territory** to help **other sloths** to **find them,** especially **females** looking for a **mate.** After all, we all want to find that **special someone** who we can **fall in love** with.

A sloth's weekly **adventure** may produce a **poo** shaped like a **rotten banana,** but is it **possible** that **YOU** might have more in **common** with a **banana** than you thought?

73

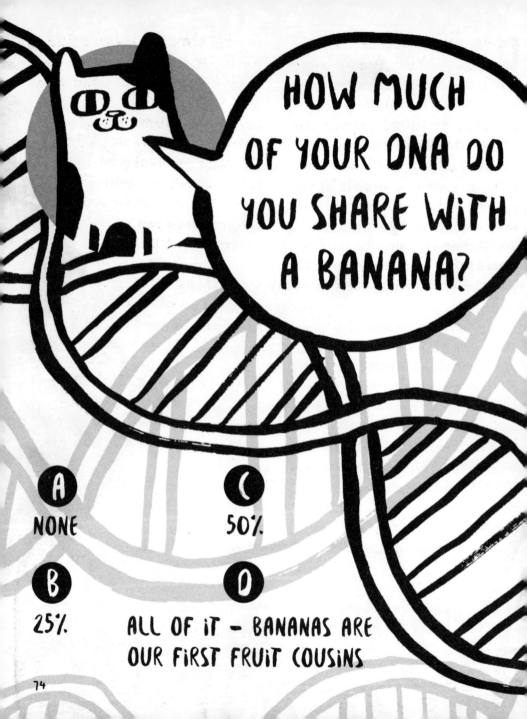

DNA is the **material** that makes you **YOU**. It determines a **lot of things** about you, such as the **colour of your eyes**, the **type of blood** you have, the **shape of your face** and the **curliness of your hair.** Your DNA even determines whether or not you can **roll your tongue!** And some other **strange** things too, like whether you enjoy the taste of **coriander** or whether, like **me**, you think it tastes of **soap.** Yuck.

Your DNA sits inside **every cell** of your body, where it makes up your **genes.** (These are not to be confused with the **blue skinny things** that your big sister wears on the weekends, those are her **jeans**.) Each gene is a **set of instructions,** containing the **information** your body needs in order to make a particular type of **protein** – just like a **recipe** contains all the information you need to bake a **chocolate cake.** Mmm.

Like all other **humans**, you have a **full set** of more than **20,000 genes** inside **every cell** of your body, and each set consists of enough recipes to make **every protein** your body could possibly need. This means that just **one** of your tiny cells could tell us pretty much **everything about you.** Even a cell in your **little toe.** But the **clever** thing is, **THAT** cell **knows where it is,** and so inside it only the genes with instructions relevant to **little toes** are **switched on,** while the **rest of the genes** – such as ones relevant to **hearts** or **eyeballs** – are **switched off.**

THE AVERAGE HUMAN HAS OVER 30 TRILLION CELLS IN THEIR BODY.

Your genes **work together with your environment** to make you **who you are.** For example, your genes might give you **naturally blonde hair**, but you might decide to **dye it brown.** Or **purple.** Similarly, you might have the sort of genes that should make you **grow six feet tall**, but if you don't get enough **healthy food** to eat when you're **young**, you may **not quite make it.** Or your genes might give you a **brain** that naturally **learns best** in a certain way, such as by **reading about things** or by **writing them down**, but the more you **study** or **try out new stuff**, the more your brain will **learn and improve**. Just like a muscle, your brain gets **stronger** the more you use it.

You **inherit** your DNA from your **biological parents.** In other words, the parents who produced the **egg** and **sperm** cells that made the **embryo** that eventually turned into **YOU.** (These might not **necessarily** be the parents who are bringing you up.) This means that **half** of the DNA in **each** of your cells originally came from each of your **biological parents.** That's why you probably **look quite a bit like** anyone else who also came from the **same** biological parents as you, like your full or half **brothers or sisters** (your **siblings**).

However, even **full** siblings don't look **quite the same** as each other. This is because **each sibling** has a slightly different

76

random combination of DNA from each of their parents. So, while your sister's DNA will certainly be more similar to **your DNA** than to the DNA of, say, the **annoying lady** in the supermarket, there'll still be lots of **differences** between you. In fact, **everyone's** DNA is **totally unique.** That's how **the police** can use the DNA left behind at the **scene of a crime** – found in a **stray hair,** a **spot of blood** or even a **fingernail** – to identify someone.

Alright clever clogs, not **EVERYONE'S** DNA is totally unique. **Identical twins** have **exactly the same** DNA as one other, because they were made from the **SAME** original **sperm** and **egg** cell. When the **embryo** started to **develop** in the **womb,** it **split** in half leaving

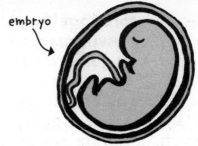
embryo

two identical embryos ... which eventually made two identical babies.

This means that the only **differences** between identical twins are the things that are influenced by their **environment,** such as what they **eat,** what they read or learn and how they are **treated.** This is why identical twins might have **quite different personalities** or interests and might be **good at different subjects** at school. But their DNA remains **identical.** So, if you happen to have an **identical twin** and you want to **commit a crime,** you could easily **trick** the police into thinking **your twin did it.** But please don't tell them I **told you** to do that.

ANYWAY, WHAT'S ALL THIS GOT TO DO WITH BANANAS?

Well, as I said **earlier**, you **inherited** your genes from your **biological parents** and they inherited **their** genes from **their** biological parents (your **grandparents**) and your grandparents inherited **their** genes from **THEIR** biological parents (your **great**-grandparents) ... and so on and so on. This means that you will have some of the **same genes** as your great-great-great-grandparents. And so will approximately **1,000** other people on the planet ... who have the **SAME** great-great-great-grandparents

as you! This bunch of people are actually your **fourth cousins**, although it's pretty unlikely that you **know** many of them. But you all share a **common ancestor** and therefore also share some **genes**.

If we go just **two generations** further back than that, not only do you have some of the **same genes** as your great-great-great-great-great-grandparents (who were probably your age around **200**

78

years ago), but so do a whopping **174,000** of your **sixth cousins.** Good thing you won't need to invite them all round for a **family dinner.** Or remember their **birthdays.**

Now, if we were to **keep** going back **hundreds of thousands** of years, we could probably trace some of your DNA back to your **early human ancestors**. In fact, it's likely that around

3–4 million years ago there lived a **human-like creature** that carried some of your genes and was a **common ancestor** to you ... and to **every other human** alive today. So, on some level, we're **ALL related.**

This is getting kinda **silly** now, but if we went back about **500 million years,** through your **ape-like** ancestors and beyond, we would probably come across one of **your earliest ancestors**. A glorious ... **primeval worm**. It is thought that this rather **strange-looking** grandparent of yours (and mine), that was no bigger than a **grain of rice,** is likely to have been the **common ancestor** not just to **all humans and apes,** but also to **all modern animals!** This means that **cute kittens** and **boring old beetles,** along with everything in between, are probably your **hundredth millionth cousins.**

Let's go **even further** back ... to **1.6 billion** years ago. (Take a deep breath, we're nearly there now.) Around this time, there lived an **organism** that was a **common ancestor** to all modern animals **AND PLANTS**. Yep. An ancestor that gave rise not just to humans, monkeys, killer whales, butterflies and hummingbirds, but also to oak trees, daffodils, banana trees ... and **bananas**. This means that your great-great-great-great-great (and an **awful lot** more greats) grandparents were **the same** as those of a ... wait for it ... **banana**. Uh huh.

Let's call this **ancient creature** a **planimal** (don't try and find this in a **dictionary**, I just made it up). Now, as our planimal ancestors **reproduced**, their **descendants** began to separate into **different groups** (or **kingdoms**). As this happened, some **key differences** evolved between the kingdoms. **New versions of genes** appeared that helped species to be **better adapted** to their **surroundings** – so they were more likely to **survive**. This is what's known as **evolution**.

For example, **plants** evolved to be able to **trap light** using a **green pigment** called chlorophyll, so that they could use its energy to make **sugar** through **photosynthesis** (and we've already talked about how important that is for

their survival). On the other hand, animals evolved to be able to **walk** or **swim** or **fly,** but were unable to **make their own sugar** so they had to rely on **plants** for **food.** That's why plants are usually **green** but animals don't tend to be. (OK except **parrots.** And **grasshoppers.** And ... OK **FINE!**

But you get my point.)

However, although plants and animals evolved to have **many different genes,** they also **kept** hold of a lot of the **SAME genes** from their common planimal ancestor. But **why?**

It might not have **occurred** to you, but although humans are obviously **quite different** to plants in **many ways,** humans and plants do actually have **some important similarities.**

For example, like all **plants,** humans and animals are **made up of cells.** Therefore, you and plants – including your **bendy banana buddies** – need **genes** that carry the **basic instructions** for how to **build** these cells. You and plants also need genes that tell you **how to grow,** how to **produce energy,** how to **become yellow** (OK, so that bit's **not true**) and even how to **make babies.** The **bottom line** is that, whilst you might **LOOK** pretty different to your **fruity yellow cousins,** you might be surprised to know that about **half** of your DNA is **the same.**

THE **ANSWER** is (
YOU SHARE 50% OF YOUR DNA WITH A BANANA.

If human genes are that similar to those of our **legless bendy friends,** just how similar must we be to creatures who not only **have legs** like ours, but also have **hearts** and **eyes** and **ears** too?! Yep, **pretty similar.** Humans share around **60%** of our DNA with both **flies** and **chickens, 70%** with **worms** and **slugs, 80%** with **cows, 90%** with **cats** ... and a whopping great **99%** with our closest living non-human relatives, **chimpanzees.**

And as for our **fellow human beings,** whilst **some people** seem to spend a long time focusing on the **differences between us** – be that the **colour of** **our skin,** the **shape of our noses,** the **size of our muscles** or the **people we choose to love** – it's worth **remembering** that, when we scratch beneath the **surface,** our DNA is actually **99.9% identical** to that of **all other humans.**

Whilst we might all be pretty much **the same** when it comes to our **genes,** what makes us all different is the **choices** we make and the way we **live our lives.** Although we can't choose our **genes,** we can choose to make **good decisions.** Speaking of which, did you know there's something **YOU** can do to help you make **BETTER** decisions?

YOU WILL PROBABLY MAKE BETTER DECISIONS WHEN YOU ...

A ARE HUNGRY

B ARE TIRED

C NEED A WEE

D HAVE JUST BEEN STUNG BY A WASP

If I were to offer you a bar of your favourite **chocolate RIGHT NOW**, but then said, "Actually, if you can **wait until tomorrow**, I will give **£10 instead**" - what would you do?

Admittedly, if the bar of chocolate were the **size of your dog**, then I wouldn't **blame you** if you just wanted to start **scoffing** it. However - assuming it was a pretty **standard-sized** bar - even though **devouring** the bar **immediately** would no-doubt result in a whole heap of **instant happiness,** just **think** how many **MORE** chocolate bars (or other far more **sensible** things) you could **buy** tomorrow if you **waited** for that £10 instead.

In other words, **resisting the urge** for **instant gratification** would give you a much greater chance of even **more** heavenly joy in the **LONG-TERM.**

But, whilst it's pretty clear that **waiting** until tomorrow would be the **BETTER** decision (ignoring the **damage** that all that chocolate might do to your **teeth**), it certainly wouldn't be an **EASY** one to **make**. Let's face it - when presented with a **mouth-watering** bar of **chocolatey goodness**, it's pretty unlikely you'd be able to think beyond the **first mouthful,** let alone as far ahead as **tomorrow.**

So, what might **HELP** you to make this **difficult**, but ultimately **better**, decision?

Well, some **scientists** attempted to find out the **answer** to this question by doing a similar kind of **experiment** with a group of **volunteers**. Bizarrely, they found that when the volunteers **needed a wee** they were more likely to **resist** the **temptation** of instant gratification and make a decision with a **better long-term outcome**.

THE ANSWER is C
YOU WILL PROBABLY MAKE BETTER DECISIONS WHEN YOU NEED A WEE.

But why does this happen? Well, when you **need a wee,** the part of your brain responsible for **bladder-control** kicks in, controlling the **physical urge** to just ... let it all out and **wee on the floor**. You are probably pretty **good** at controlling this urge. Well, **most** of the time anyway.

Interestingly, scientists believe that the **same** part of your brain is responsible for controlling your **emotional urges** too – like the **urge** to just eat that bar of chocolate **RIGHT NOW**. This would explain why, when you need a wee, you might be more able to **control** your desire for **instant pleasure** and instead make a better **long-term** decision. In fact, several **world leaders** (including former UK prime minister David Cameron) have admitted to using this **'full-bladder technique'** to maintain **focus** and **clarity** during their **speeches** and **negotiations**.

Maybe that's why **department stores** usually have **lots of toilets** – they **WANT** you to do lots of **wees** so you have an **empty bladder**. After all, if you **needed a wee** when you were out **shopping,** you might be **stopped** from following your **emotional urges** that tell you to ask your mum for that extra **LEGO® set** that you don't really **NEED**. Or yet another **trampoline**. I mean, where exactly are you going to **put it?!**

Apart from the **cost** of buying new things (and the fact that another trampoline simply won't fit in your tiny garden), why might it be a **better decision** not to keep buying **new stuff** that you don't actually need?

When you buy something **new** from a big **high street shop** or an **online giant,** the chances are that it has probably been made in a **factory** in another part of the world. These factories get their **energy** by burning **fossil fuels,** such as **coal, oil** and **gas.** And burning fossil fuels pumps **carbon dioxide** into our **atmosphere,** which is really bad for our **planet** because it's causing **climate change.**

SUNLIGHT

HEAT

Why is it important we understand about climate change?? **Well,** one of my **favourite** things about **science** is that we can use it to **learn more** about our planet. And when we **understand** the planet, we can help to **change it** for the **better.** Learning about **climate change** might feel like **getting bad news,** but actually the fact that we **already know** so much about it is **really GOOD news,** because scientists can only **figure out solutions** when we have all the **information.** So let's **find out** what's happening to our planet **together.**

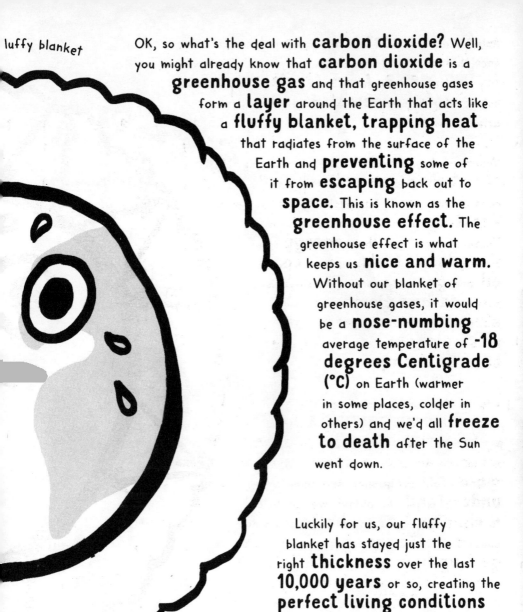

luffy blanket

OK, so what's the deal with **carbon dioxide?** Well, you might already know that **carbon dioxide** is a **greenhouse gas** and that greenhouse gases form a **layer** around the Earth that acts like a **fluffy blanket, trapping heat** that radiates from the surface of the Earth and **preventing** some of it from **escaping** back out to **space.** This is known as the **greenhouse effect.** The greenhouse effect is what keeps us **nice and warm.** Without our blanket of greenhouse gases, it would be a **nose-numbing** average temperature of **-18 degrees Centigrade (°C)** on Earth (warmer in some places, colder in others) and we'd all **freeze to death** after the Sun went down.

Luckily for us, our fluffy blanket has stayed just the right **thickness** over the last **10,000 years** or so, creating the **perfect living conditions** for humans - **nice and warm,** but not **TOO warm.**

89

Our **stable** climate has been thanks to the **carbon cycle.**

When other living creatures **feed** off these trees and other plants, they then take the carbon compounds into their **own bodies.**

In the carbon cycle, **carbon dioxide** in our atmosphere is constantly being **absorbed** into the oceans, as well as being **locked** into **carbon compounds** (such as **sugar**) in **trees** and other **plants** through **photosynthesis.**

3 Some of the carbon compounds in the plants and animals are then **turned back** into carbon dioxide, which is **released** back into the **atmosphere** – usually when the animal **breathes out** or through **tiny holes** underneath the plant's leaves called **stomata**.

The remaining carbon compounds are **stored** in the bodies of plants and animals, but are **turned back** into carbon dioxide again when the living thing **dies** and the dead matter **decays** or is **burnt**.

4

IT'S IMPORTANT TO UNDERSTAND ABOUT THESE CYCLES BECAUSE SOME PEOPLE GET CONFUSED BETWEEN THE NATURAL CHANGES IN CARBON DIOXIDE LEVELS AND THE CHANGES CAUSED BY HUMANS. SCIENTISTS ARE CERTAIN THAT THE CHANGES IN RECENT YEARS HAVE BEEN DIRECTLY CAUSED BY THE ACTIONS OF HUMANS (WE'LL TALK ABOUT WHAT SORT OF ACTIONS A BIT LATER).

The whole cycle then **starts again**.

In this way, carbon dioxide is constantly being **removed** and **replaced** in our atmosphere, which keeps the **levels** of carbon dioxide (and the **thickness** of our fluffy blanket) pretty **stable** over **thousands of years**.

However, over **MUCH LONGER** periods of time, carbon dioxide levels are also affected by the **Earth's natural cycles** ...

Natural changes in the way the Earth **travels around** the Sun lead to very **gradual changes** in the amount of **sunlight** that reaches **different parts** of the Earth. This causes the **summers** to get **cooler** in the **Northern Hemisphere**, allowing **some ice** to **survive** over the summer months. The **shiny white** ice **reflects** a lot of the **Sun's heat** back from its **surface**, causing the Earth to get even colder and **more ice** to form. This reflects more heat, which causes further cooling, which leads to more ice ... and so on and so on. This **'feedback loop'** is known as the **ice-albedo effect.**

OOH IT'S RATHER CHILLY!

In addition, as the land and oceans **cool down,** cooler oceans **absorb** more **carbon dioxide** from the atmosphere. This **reduces** the **thickness** of our fluffy blanket. A **thinner blanket** then makes the Earth cool down **EVEN MORE,** which results in the oceans getting **even colder.** The colder oceans then absorb **even more** carbon dioxide, the blanket gets **even thinner,** which makes the Earth get **even colder** ... and so on and so on.

This **second feedback loop,** and others like it, continues until the Earth gets **so cold** that much of the ocean surface **freezes over** and large **ice sheets** form on the land. In fact, nearly **a third** of the planet turns to **ice.** We have entered what is known as an **Ice Age.** The last time we entered one of these was about **100,000 years ago,** long before humans were around.

93

After a bone-chilling **90,000 years** or so of **freezing temperatures,** the Earth's **orbit** around the Sun is nearly back to the **beginning of its cycle**. As a result, the amount of **sunlight** reaching different parts of the Earth **changes** again, causing the **summers** in the northern hemisphere to get **warmer.** Therefore, the chilly oceans start to **warm** back up, causing the **sea ice** and **land ice** to begin to **melt.**

As the oceans warm and the sea ice melts, **carbon dioxide** is released back into the atmosphere and our fluffy blanket begins to get **thicker** again. The planet **warms even more,** increasing the temperature of the **oceans** and melting **even more ice,** which releases **even more carbon dioxide,** thickening our blanket **further.** Eventually, the planet becomes warm enough for pretty much **all the ice to melt** – except at the two **poles** and high up on the **mountains.** The Ice Age is **over at last.** Phew.

The blanket of carbon dioxide should then stay roughly the **same thickness** for around **10,000 years** or so, kept in check by the **carbon cycle** that we talked about earlier, and this keeps the Earth **nice and warm** ... until the planet's orbit cycle **begins again** and we start heading towards our **NEXT** Ice Age.

What we've seen here is that these **NATURAL** cycles of changes in **carbon dioxide levels** take place **INCREDIBLY SLOWLY.** Over **THOUSANDS OF YEARS.** And as we've already learned, that's **nothing like** what's happening **today.**

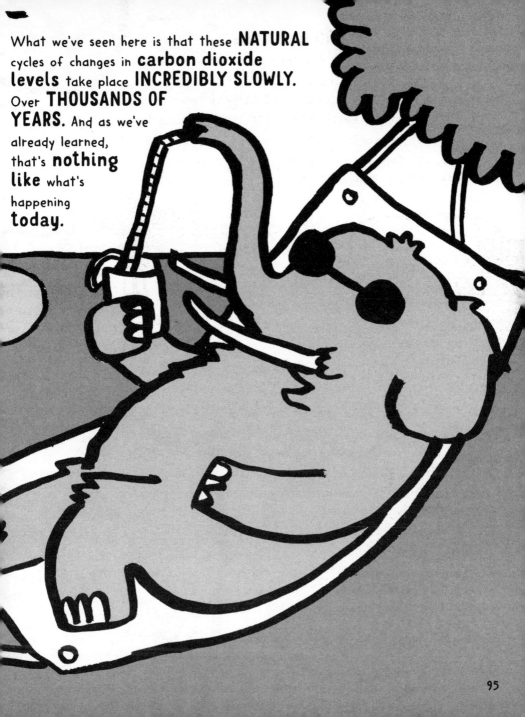

SO, WHAT IS HAPPENING TODAY?

Well, about **11,700 years ago** we came out of our last **Ice Age.** For a **long time** our fluffy blanket remained roughly the **same thickness** making the atmosphere **nice and warm** and creating just the right **conditions** for humans to be able to **settle** and **farm.**

Then, around **5,000 years ago,** the Earth began to enter its next **natural cycle.** Changes in the Earth's orbit caused the temperature to start to **very slowly fall** again, which **SHOULD** mean that we're heading very slowly towards our **next Ice Age.** I say **SHOULD,** because you're probably aware that that's not what's **actually** happening. Instead, the Earth is heating up ... because humans **got in the way.**

You see, a few thousand years ago humans started **interfering** with the **carbon cycle.** Without **realising** what they were doing, they started **THICKENING** our blanket.

Secondly, in the place of forests, humans planted **paddy fields** to grow **rice**. The problem is, paddy fields have **waterlogged soils** that are prime conditions for certain types of **microbes** to grow. And these microbes release **methane** – a powerful **greenhouse gas**.

Thirdly, they started **breeding cows** for **milk** and **meat**. And cows have those same types of microbes in their **stomachs** helping them to **digest grass**, so they produce a huge amount of **methane** in their **burps** (and a bit in their **farts**).

Firstly, they **cut down trees** so they could clear land for **farming**, or so they could use the wood for **building things** or **making paper**, or **burn it** to keep **warm**. This is known as **deforestation**, and it **reduced** the amount of **carbon dioxide** that was being **removed** from the blanket because there were fewer trees to absorb it.

The **extra** greenhouse gases produced by these human activities made our blanket get a little **thicker**, **warming** us up a bit and **balancing out** the **drop** in temperature caused by the changes in the Earth's **orbit**. This meant that for a **long time** the temperature on Earth remained **pretty constant**, only cooling slightly. Until something **BIG** happened. Something that would change **EVERYTHING** ... We discovered **fossil fuels**.

Since the start of the **Industrial Revolution** in the late **1700s**, humans have been burning huge quantities of these **fossil fuels** – such as **coal, oil** and **natural gas** – to release **energy**. This energy is very **useful,** for powering heavy machinery in factories, heating our homes, driving cars and trains, or generating electricity.

So what's the problem with **burning fossil fuels?**

Well, fossil fuels contain the remnants of **dead plants** and **sea creatures** that have been **trapped underground** for **millions of years**. And these remnants contain **CARBON.** When fossil fuels are **burned,** the **trapped carbon** is turned into **carbon dioxide ... LOTS OF IT.** And this carbon dioxide is released into the **atmosphere.** Uh oh. Nobody **knew it** at the time, but all of a sudden, our fluffy blanket started to get **A LOT THICKER** ... and **VERY, VERY QUICKLY.**

You see, everyone thought it was a **good decision** to burn fossil fuels, as the energy they released made **people's lives better.** But they didn't know what the **long-term consequences** would be. Now, thanks to scientists **studying the world,** we know that different **decisions** need to be made. By becoming a scientist, **YOU** could help the **whole world** make **better decisions** in the future, whether or not they **need a wee!**

Oi! YOU'RE BURNING MY ANCESTORS!

But the **burning of fossil fuels** isn't the **only big change** that has taken place. Since the **Industrial Revolution** humans have also been chopping down **ever-increasing** numbers of trees. In fact, over the past 150 years, our planet has lost a staggering **1.5 trillion trees** – that's nearly a **quarter** of the trees that were once on our Earth. This was mostly been to clear space for the **crops** that **feed** us and produce substances such as **palm oil** (which is found in many types of soap, shampoo, chocolate, bread and crisps) and to make room for the ever increasing number of **livestock,** especially **cows** – not to mention the huge amount of land that is needed to **grow crops** to **feed** these cows. Today, in the Amazon rainforest an area of forest as large as **three football fields** is being destroyed **EVERY MINUTE.**

BUT WHAT DOES CHOPPING DOWN TREES HAVE TO DO WITH THE THICKNESS OF OUR FLUFFY BLANKET?

THAT WAS WHERE I USED TO SLEEP!

Well, not only does deforestation mean there are **fewer trees** around to **remove** all that **excess carbon dioxide** from the atmosphere, but also, when chopped down trees are **burned**, the carbon that has been **stored** in their trunks for **tens** or even **hundreds** of years is released **BACK** into the atmosphere. Double whammy. (Not to mention the fact that trees provide us with **food, medicines** and **fuels**, they **protect** us from **floods** and **storms** and they are the **habitats** of countless **wild creatures**.)

Fortunately, if chopped down trees are **left to rot** instead of being burned, their **carbon** ends up being **stored** in the **soil** (along with carbon from the bodies of other **dead plants** and **animals**) instead of being released into the air as **carbon dioxide**. Phew. But the problem is, since the Industrial Revolution our **carbon-rich soils** have been getting increasingly **damaged** by **modern intensive farming** practices, which means that lots of carbon that had been stored **in the soil** has been being **turned back** into carbon dioxide. So our blanket has been getting **EVEN THICKER.** Plus, these **modern farming methods** use **chemical fertilisers** that release another extremely potent greenhouse gas, **nitrous oxide.**

In addition, over the years farmers have been breeding **more and MORE cows** for the meat and dairy industries, and, as we know, **COWS** produce huge amounts of the greenhouse gas **methane** in their burps – and their **waste** also produces **nitrous oxide.**

As a direct result of all these **human actions,** scientists have now **confirmed** that over the past 150 years the levels of **greenhouse gases** in our atmosphere have been **shooting up** at an **alarming rate.** In fact, over the past **60 years** carbon dioxide levels have been rising at least **100 TIMES FASTER** than any of the **NATURAL** changes that brought us out of the **Ice Ages.** As a result, our fluffy blanket has been getting **far, far thicker** than it **should be** – and than it **has been** for a **VERY** long time.

In fact, today, the levels of carbon dioxide in our atmosphere are **higher** than they have been in a staggering **THREE MILLION YEARS.**

WHAT HAS THIS SUPER-THICK BLANKET BEEN DOING TO OUR PLANET?

Well, at a time when the Earth should have been **slowly cooling down** and heading towards an Ice Age, instead we have been **steadily HEATING UP.** This is known as **global warming**.

You might have **noticed** it yourself. Shockingly, all 20 of the **hottest years on record** have occurred since 1998. The years 2016 and 2020 were the joint hottest years **EVER RECORDED**, while in 2019 nearly **400 temperature records** were broken across 29 countries. As I am sitting here **writing** this book, records show that **July 2019** was the **hottest month ever.** By the time you are **reading** this book, those records may well have been **broken.**

Gosh, what a lot of **terrible decisions** we made about **fossil fuels, forests** and **farming,** causing **major damage** to our planet because we simply **didn't know better.** But the **good news** is that now we **DO** know, we can make **new decisions** that stop the damage from **getting any worse** – and **YOU** can be part of that.

By the way, I'm aware that it may seem **pretty chilly** where you are **right now.** This is because some areas of the world are heating up **less than others.** There can also be short-term **dips** in temperature too, due to changes in the **weather.** But the important point is that, **overall,** and in the **long-term,** the planet is **warming.**

The Earth's **atmosphere** is now a whopping great ...
1°C warmer than it was 150 years ago.

Wait a minute, **1°C?!**

OK, **1°C** might not **sound like much,** but the Earth is **so huge** that it takes an **enormous** amount of **energy** to **warm it up** by even a **tiny** amount. And so that 1°C represents an **AWFUL LOT** of extra **heat energy.** Our planet has almost certainly not been **this hot** for at least **100,000 years** – long before **human civilisation** began.

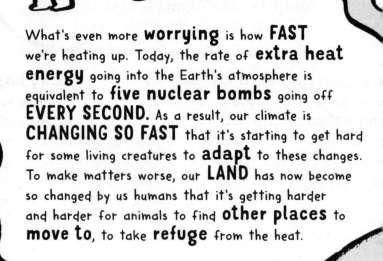

What's even more **worrying** is how **FAST** we're heating up. Today, the rate of **extra heat energy** going into the Earth's atmosphere is equivalent to **five nuclear bombs** going off **EVERY SECOND.** As a result, our climate is **CHANGING SO FAST** that it's starting to get hard for some living creatures to **adapt** to these changes. To make matters worse, our **LAND** has now become so changed by us humans that it's getting harder and harder for animals to find **other places** to **move to**, to take **refuge** from the heat.

All this **extra heat** is causing **major problems,** such as **melting ice caps, rising sea levels** and **damage to wildlife,** as well as changes to our **climate** that can result in the **spread of diseases** and **extreme weather** such as heatwaves, forest fires, droughts, storms and floods. Such events can not only **damage our homes, affect our health** and **harm our wildlife,** but they can also prevent the **crops that feed** us from being able to **grow.**

You've probably **heard** that stuff like this is **already happening** in many parts of the world today. Perhaps you or your family have already been **impacted** by them? But the worrying thing is, as temperatures continue to rise, they'll become **more and more common.** Even if you're lucky enough to **escape** the **direct impacts** of these events, remember most of us depend on food that's been **imported** from other parts of the world; so if **crops** are damaged by extreme weather events **far away,** that's likely to lead to **price rises** or even **shortages of certain foods where YOU are too.**

That's why it is so **important** that we now all **work together** and make good decisions to try to stop the atmosphere from getting **any hotter** than it already is. Children are the world's most **precious** and **valuable** resource. **YOU** can help change the future of the planet!

SAVE THE PLANET

THE UK GETS AROUND 50% OF ITS FOOD FROM OTHER COUNTRIES, INCLUDING AROUND 70-80% OF ITS FRUIT AND VEGETABLES.

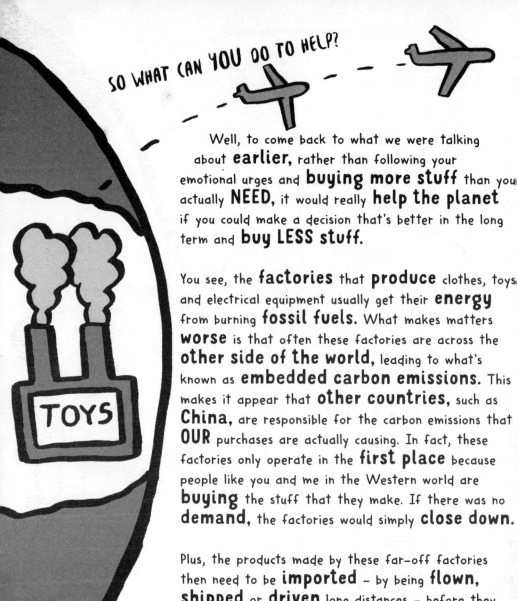

SO WHAT CAN YOU DO TO HELP?

Well, to come back to what we were talking about **earlier**, rather than following your emotional urges and **buying more stuff** than you actually **NEED**, it would really **help the planet** if you could make a decision that's better in the long term and **buy LESS stuff**.

You see, the **factories** that **produce** clothes, toys and electrical equipment usually get their **energy** from burning **fossil fuels**. What makes matters **worse** is that often these factories are across the **other side of the world**, leading to what's known as **embedded carbon emissions**. This makes it appear that **other countries**, such as **China**, are responsible for the carbon emissions that **OUR** purchases are actually causing. In fact, these factories only operate in the **first place** because people like you and me in the Western world are **buying** the stuff that they make. If there was no **demand**, the factories would simply **close down**.

Plus, the products made by these far-off factories then need to be **imported** – by being **flown, shipped** or **driven** long distances – before they make it to our **shops** or **homes**. And I'm sure you know that planes, ferries and lorries burn **fossil fuels**, pumping out **EVEN MORE** carbon dioxide.

By the time you get to **wear** or **use** something new, each item that you buy will probably have caused the release of **an awful lot** of carbon dioxide into our atmosphere.

> THE AMOUNT OF CARBON DIOXIDE EMISSIONS THAT YOU ARE PERSONALLY RESPONSIBLE FOR IS CALLED YOUR CARBON FOOTPRINT.

So next time you're about to buy something new, it's good to **ask yourself:** do you really NEED it? Or could you just as easily **do without it** or get something similar **second-hand?** Perhaps you could even try **holding in your wee** so you're less **tempted** by the **instant gratification** of buying something that you know, **deep down,** you don't really need.

Making good **shopping decisions** is one important thing that you and your **family** can do to help **slow down** the dangerous **heating** of our planet. I'll be talking about some **other** things you can do later in this book.

But for now, I think you should **congratulate** yourself on having just learned a **huge chunk** of **important science** about what's happening to our planet. You might even know **more** about **climate change** than your **parents** and **teachers** right now, and they might be asking you **all about it** later.

Some of what you've learned might have felt **scary** or **upsetting,** but don't forget that **knowledge** is the first step towards **changing the world.** Even though us humans have **damaged our planet** without realising it, life is a bit like **science.** And in science it's OK to find out you **got something wrong,** as long as you **learn from it** and then **change what you do.** And that's what we, as a **planet,** need to do now so that we can start to **build** a **better future.**

BUT FIRST, WHY DON'T WE MOVE ONTO SOMETHING A BIT LESS SERIOUS. TALKING OF BUILDING OUR FUTURE, DID YOU KNOW THAT THERE'S AN ANIMAL THAT DOES SUCH STRANGE-SHAPED POOS THAT IT COULD PROBABLY BUILD ITS OWN HOUSE OUT OF THEM?

It might surprise you to know that there is an animal out there whose poo forms **perfect little cubes.** (Yeah yeah, I know that's not strictly **'square-shaped'** poos, it's poos with square-shaped **sides,** but you know what I mean.)

From the pongy list of **poopers** on page 109, you might have already guessed that the animal **LEAST** likely to do a perfectly **cube-shaped** poo is going to be ... a **whale.**

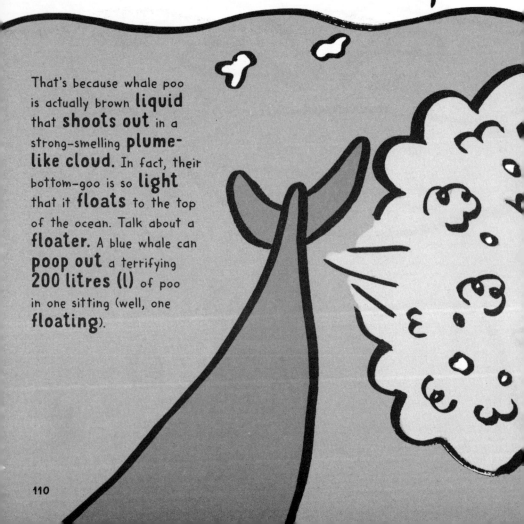

That's because whale poo is actually brown **liquid** that **shoots out** in a strong-smelling **plume-like cloud.** In fact, their bottom-goo is so **light** that it **floats** to the top of the ocean. Talk about a **floater.** A blue whale can **poop out** a terrifying **200 litres (l)** of poo in one sitting (well, one **floating**).

Some whales use their mega poo-cloud to **protect** themselves when they feel threatened. In 2015, a Canadian diver got caught up in a huge **expulsion** of poo that he described as a **'poopnado'** from a giant **sperm whale.** After it had finished doing its **business,** which took several minutes, the whale **bobbed** up and down and **splashed** its tail around so much that the ball of poo-goo became a kind of **giant brown cloud** that the whale could **hide** inside. Then, the whale **burst** out of it and **disappeared** down into the **depths.**

Whales only **poo** when they're **close to the surface** of the ocean. This is because when they **dive,** their **non-essential** bodily functions **shut down** so they can **focus** on the dive. Kinda like how you don't accidentally **poop one out** when you're in the middle of a game of **football.** Although actually, poor old **Gary Lineker** did that once during a **World Cup** match.

Anyway, the whale's **floating poo-bath** is very useful to **other creatures** living **near the surface** of the sea, as it is full of **nitrogen** and **iron** from the food that the whale ate when it was **deep** on a dive. By bringing **deep-sea nutrients** to the **surface** of the water, whales provide food for tiny **sea plants** known as **phytoplankton** (also known as **algae**) so their populations can **flourish.**

Lots of sea creatures **feed off** algae, and lots of other creatures **feed off** THOSE creatures, which means that humble **whale poo** helps **entire marine ecosystems.** (An ecosystem is a **community** of living things that share the same **physical environment** and **depend** on one another to **survive**). That's why whales are sometimes described as 'ecosystem engineers'.

Algae carry out **photosynthesis,** which means that, as well as being the **food** for many other sea creatures, they are also an important **carbon sink.** Carbon sinks are man-made or natural things such as trees, plants, soil and the oceans (and algae) that **absorb and store** more **carbon dioxide** from the atmosphere than they release. In fact, plants in the Antarctic Ocean **soak up** more than **twice as much** carbon dioxide as the **Amazon rainforest!**

Given that algae get their **nutrients** from **whale poo,** it is estimated that, in the Antarctic Ocean alone, poo from **sperm whales** is responsible for the storage of an almighty

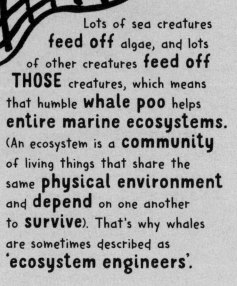

TODAY'S SPECIAL

free-range
whale-poo-fed
plankton

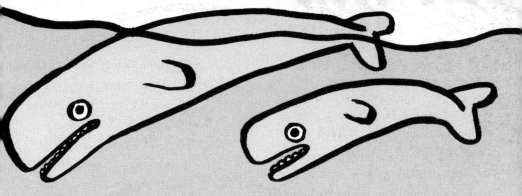

200,000 **tonnes** of carbon dioxide every year.

The **bottom** line is that **whales** are not only beautiful, they are **really important** too, so we should **look after them.** However, over the past **100 years** or so there has sadly been a **catastrophic decline** in whale numbers, with some species becoming **endangered.** This is mostly because whales have been **hunted** for their **fatty blubber,** which can be boiled down to produce **soap** and **margarine.** During the **20th century,** more than

1.5 million whales were killed by hunters in the Antarctic Ocean and blue whales virtually **disappeared** from there. Luckily, since 1967, commercial whale hunting has been **banned** in most countries and recent **surveys** show that the numbers of Antarctic blue whales — as well as humpbacks and other whales in this area — are finally **going up again.**

Although there are still many whale populations **under threat** across the world, due to **climate change, pollution** and **overfishing,** this story gives us **hope** that humans **CAN** have a **positive impact** on the natural world when we **really try.**

Anyway, back to the more **bizarre** matter of **square-sided** poos ...

If whales are out of the running, then **who** might be our most likely **cube-pooer?** Let's consider the other options ...

Bears do large **cylindrical sausage-shaped** poos – they're kinda like human poos but much **fatter** and can be up to **30 centimetres (cm) long.** That's probably longer than your **forearm.** I wouldn't want to fall **face down** onto one of those **squelchers** in the woods, would **you?**

Fox droppings, on the other hand, look like **small skinny sausages** – perhaps a bit like mini chipolatas. They are only 5–7 cm long, with **pointy** ends.

That leaves us with ... the **wombat.** Wombats are small **furry** creatures that live in Australia. They have short legs and stubby tails ... and their poos are shaped like **perfect little cubes.**

THE **ANSWER** is **B**
A WOMBAT DOES
SQUARE-SHAPED POOS.

Does this mean that wombats have **square-shaped bottoms?** Sadly not. A wombat's anus is **round,** just like yours or mine (or a bear's or a fox's). You'd think that a round anus ought to **sculpt** the wombat's poo into **little cylinders** as it pops out, right? So then why on Earth does it pop out in **cubes?**

Experts have found that it's the combination of the **dryness** of the wombat's poo and the **elasticity** (stretchiness) of their **intestines** that gives a wombat's poo this **unusual** shape.

Wombats have the **driest** poo of all mammals. This makes sense as they live in very **hot, dry areas,** so they need to **keep hold** of as much **water** as possible. Their poo stays in their **digestive tract** for up to **18 days,** during which time most of the water is **sucked back** into their bodies. It's thought that **ridges** inside the wombat's **intestines** might **sculpt** the super-dry poo into **rectangles** (OK, rectangular prisms, smarty-poo-pants) and that the **varied stretchiness** of the intestine wall might help further **mould** it into **cubes.** By the time they are ready to **pop out,** the wombat's poo-cubes are so **dry and hard** that even the wombat's round anus **can't** round their **edges.**

What I love most about **science** is that most things happen for a **reason**. Things tend to **make sense**. So **WHY** might having cube-shaped poo be **useful** to these little Aussie fluffy guys?

Well, like many **mammals,** wombats use their poo to **mark their territory.** For other animals it is helpful that their poo tends to be **soft and sticky** because this means it **stays where it's put** – well, **plopped**. However, a wombat's poo is so **light and dry** that it could easily just **roll away** down a **hill**. Or **blow away** in the **breeze.** Experts think that a wombat's intestines might have **evolved** to produce this unusual **flat-bottomed poop** so that it has more chance of **staying in one place.** Clever, huh?

Plus, **cubes** – like bricks – are also easy to **stack.** And wombats have been seen **piling up** their poo cubes, one on top of each other. It's thought that the **higher** the stack, the better the wombat is able to **communicate** with and **attract** other wombats. Perhaps this even helps to **protect** them from predators?

Speaking of which, did you know that there is a creature that has a rather unusual way of **scaring off** its predators?

WHICH DISGUSTING CREATURE VOMITS TO SCARE AWAY ITS PREDATORS?

A. A VULTURE

B. A WOLF

C. A RACCOON

D. A HYENA

YOU have almost certainly **vomited** at some point. Most of us have. Whether it was from eating too much **food**, reading a **book** in the back of the **car**, spinning around on a **fairground ride** or eating something **dodgy**.

Throwing up is your body's way of getting rid of **undigested** food by simply **emptying out** the contents of your stomach, the **same way** they came in.

What might **cause** this to happen? Sometimes it's because **nerves** in your **stomach** have **sensed** that it's getting too **full**. Or nerves in your **gut** have sensed that your gut is **irritated** by a **virus**, a **bacterial infection** or **eating** a certain type of **food**. Sometimes it's because **nerves** in your **inner ear** have detected that you are feeling **dizzy, seasick** or **carsick**. Or the **trigger** can come from your **central nervous system** in response to you feeling some **intense emotion,** such as fear, grief or disgust. Occasionally, you might be sick because your **brain** has detected that you've had a **bump** on the head.

Whatever the **trigger** – and **wherever** it comes from – in the end your **brain** will receive the **vomit-inducing** signal from your **nerves.** It will then send an **electrical impulse** along **another** set of nerves to the **muscles** in your **diaphragm** and your **stomach wall.** These then **contract** to **propel** your **partially-digested** food – along with some terrible-tasting, foul-smelling **acidic stomach juices** – up your **food pipe** (properly known as your **oesophagus**) and out of your mouth.

Unlike us humans, **hyenas** are rather **partial** to vomit. Especially **their own**. They even love to **roll around** in it. Gross. Exactly **why** these disgusting creatures enjoy sliding around in a **stinky puddle** of undigested hoof, bone and hair no one really knows.

Some animals, however, have found a rather more **important** use for their vomit.

EWWW!

Take the **turkey vulture**. When a **predator**, such as a **raccoon**, approaches and tries to raid the vulture's **nest full of eggs**, the protective vulture simply **coughs up** a stinky lump of semi-digested meat onto the ground. Not only does the **foul stench** of the vulture's vomit make the pesky raccoon want to run **for the hills**, but the **acid** in the vomit will **sting like crazy** if it gets into the raccoon's **face** or **eyes**.

If a predator such as a **hawk** or **eagle** is coming after the vulture **itself**, vomiting up its **last meal** can also make the vulture a great deal **lighter**, so it can **fly away** more easily.

THE **ANSWER** is **A**
A VULTURE VOMITS TO
SCARE AWAY ITS PREDATORS.

Vultures have another rather **disgusting** habit. In order to **cool down**, vultures **wee and poo** ... on their own legs. Yep. The **evaporation** of water from their **stinky excretions** removes **heat energy** from their legs, plus the high **acid** content kills any **bacteria** they may have picked up whilst **wading around** in the **rotting carcasses** of their prey.

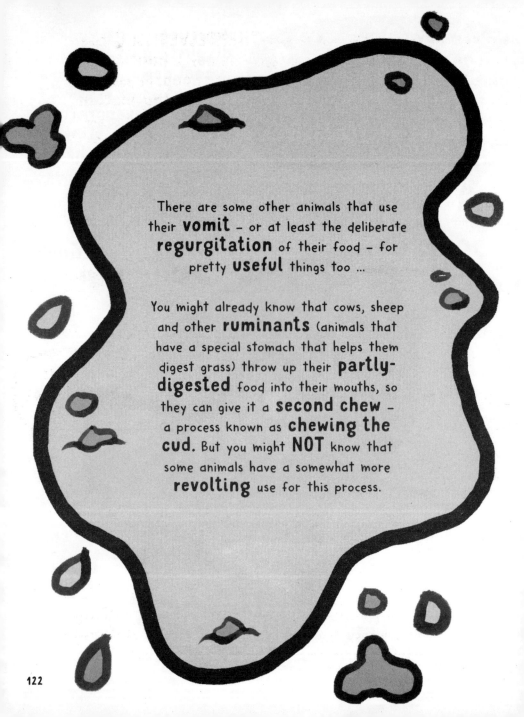

There are some other animals that use their **vomit** – or at least the deliberate **regurgitation** of their food – for pretty **useful** things too ...

You might already know that cows, sheep and other **ruminants** (animals that have a special stomach that helps them digest grass) throw up their **partly-digested** food into their mouths, so they can give it a **second chew** – a process known as **chewing the cud.** But you might **NOT** know that some animals have a somewhat more **revolting** use for this process.

Wolves use regurgitation, not to feed **THEMSELVES,** but to feed their **babies.** When an adult wolf gets back from a **hunt** with its stomach packed full of the **meat** of a **juicy sheep,** its pups will start **licking** around its **mouth.** The strange **licking motion** causes the parent wolf to **regurgitate** its partly-digested dinner back up into its **mouth,** so it can be enjoyed by the **delighted** pups. Yum.

Maybe you can ask **your mum** to do that for you next time she comes home from a **posh restaurant?** (Actually, don't do that.)

IN 2004, A SHEEP IN NEW ZEALAND CALLED SHREK ESCAPED FROM A FARM AND SPENT 6 YEARS HIDING IN CAVES IN THE MOUNTAINS, DURING WHICH TIME HE GREW NEARLY 30 KG OF WOOL. WHEN WOLVES TRIED TO EAT THE SHAGGY CREATURE, THEIR TEETH COULDN'T GET THROUGH THE FLUFF!

YOU'RE NOT EATING ME!

Eating your **mother's vomit** may sound **revolting,** but did you know that there's a creature **whose delicious** vomit you have almost certainly **snacked** on?

WHICH CREATURE'S DELICIOUS VOMIT MIGHT ACTUALLY BE GOOD FOR YOU?

A A FLY

B A BEE

C AN EARTHWORM

D A BAT

You've probably never sat down for **breakfast** and thought you'd spread some **sticky vomit** on your **toast**. Or stir some into your **porridge**. Well, actually, you probably have ...

You might have **guessed** that what I'm talking about here is **honey**. When **honeybees** drink **nectar** from flowers it **mixes** with a special **enzyme** in what's known as their **honey stomach**. The busy bee then **vomits** the **sweet sticky mixture** back up ... as **honey**.

Making honey is not an **easy task**. An average **honeybee** will only make around **one-twelfth** of a teaspoon of honey in its **entire lifetime**. A whole **JAR** of honey requires nectar from around **3 million flowers** – and it takes an awful lot of honeybees to drink that much nectar.

When a honeybee finds a good **source of nectar** for honey-making, it buzzes straight back to the hive to tell its **honeybee friends** where it is. It does so by doing a **funny little dance** known as a '**waggle dance**'. The bee uses this strange **communication ritual** to indicate to the other honeybees **exactly where** the yummy flower was, relative to the **Sun** and to its **hive**.

TOOT, TOOT!

A QUEEN HONEYBEE MAKES A STRANGE QUACKING NOISE WHEN SHE'S READY TO HATCH FROM HER EGG. ONCE HATCHED, SHE MAKES A TOOTING SOUND TO ANNOUNCE HER ARRIVAL.

Honey doesn't just **taste yummy**, it's **good for you**. Not only is it packed full of enzymes, vitamins and minerals, honey can help soothe **sore throats** and **coughs**. Some studies suggest that certain types of honey can even reduce **inflammation** of the **gut**. Honey also contains a natural **antiseptic**. That, along with its ability to **soothe pain**, means it can be used as a **wound dressing** for cuts and burns. It can even help prevent **scars** from forming. But, whilst honey might be **rather useful**, it is pretty high in **sugar**, so it's probably best not to eat **too much** of the stuff.

Making **honey** is not the only thing that we **rely** on bees for. They also play a **huge role** in making sure we can grow **yummy crops** for people to **eat**.

THE **ANSWER** IS **B**
A BEE'S DELICIOUS VOMIT IS ACTUALLY GOOD FOR YOU.

When any type of bee **nuzzles** deep into a flower, hungry for that **sweet nectar**, they sometimes happen to pick up some sticky **pollen** on their **fluffy bodies**. This pollen is made by the **male part** of the flower, called the **anther**.

When the bee flies to the **next flower**, it may **transfer** some of this pollen from its fluffy bottom onto the **female part** of that flower, called the **stigma**. This enables **fertilisation** (the process through which new **seeds** are produced) to occur. This seed might eventually grow into a whole new **baby plant**. This **transfer** of pollen from one plant to another is known as **pollination**. Pollination is **essential**, as without it the plant can't **reproduce**.

Most of the world's **crops and other plants** depend, at least to some extent, on **animals** such as bees for **pollination** – including tomatoes, squash and berries. While there are **many** important pollinating insects, such as **beetles, hoverflies** and **butterflies**, honeybees alone carry out a whopping **80%** of crop pollination. No wonder bees have been called the most **important** living creatures on our planet.

Sadly though, the **numbers** of bees and other **pollinating insects** are **falling rapidly** in many places. This is due to a combination of **habitat loss, climate change, pollution** and the use of chemical **pesticides.** In fact, as many as **10%** of insect species may now be threatened with **extinction** and it is estimated that the numbers of **land insects** have fallen by **nearly 50%** since the 1960s – more in some places, less in others. In the Netherlands, the number of **butterflies** has fallen by an average of over **80%** in the last 130 years.

Insects might seem **small** and **insignificant,** but they play a **crucial role** in the functioning of our planet. Not only do they **pollinate** the **crops** that we eat, but they also **fertilise** the soil they grow in and protect them from **pests**. Plus, insects **decompose** dead organic matter and animal waste, and help **protect** humans and animals from disease-causing organisms.

You see, **ecosystems** are like a giant game of **Jenga** – take a few pieces out from the bottom and the whole thing could come **tumbling down.**

That's why it's so **important** that we humans **take care** of even the **tiniest** creatures.

Scientists are now **working hard** to find ways to make sure that **bees are looked after** so that – as well as carrying on producing **yummy honey** to put on our **toast** – they can keep **helping us** grow **nutritious food.** At the same time, scientists are also exploring **alternative ways** of **pollinating crops** without bees.

It's not just the loss of **small** creatures that can have **big impacts** on our ecosystems. In an ecosystem, **every single** plant and animal plays a **unique** role and each organism's role **affects** all the others. It is a **delicate balance,** which can be **thrown off** very easily by any sort of **change** – especially if that change is **big** and **fast.** But the **good news** is that that balance **CAN** be **restored,** as long as we spot the problems **in time** and **do what's needed** to help the ecosystem **heal.**

This is **exactly** what happened about **100 years ago** in a huge area of **wilderness** in the United States of America called **Yellowstone National Park.** Humans had been trying to convert some of the **wild land** to **grazing areas** for **livestock.** But wild **wolves** had been wreaking **havoc,** killing the sheep and cattle. Thinking they could quickly **solve** the problem, **hunters** came in ... and **shot** all the wolves. They didn't **realise** this would have a **huge impact** on many other creatures living in the area.

Firstly, the **elk** that would usually be eaten by the wolves **shot up** in numbers because there were no **predators** to hunt them. Lucky them. But with all those **extra elk** hanging around, many of the **young plants** and **aspen trees** in the park got **eaten.**

The elk also ate lots of the **vegetation** on the banks of the **rivers.** Consequently, the **riverbanks** started to **erode,** causing the rivers to **widen.**

There were now **fewer trees** shading the rivers, which meant that the water got **warmer.** This affected the type of fish that could **live** in the rivers.

Plus, the **songbirds** that would normally build their **nests** on the riverbank now had **nowhere** to live; so many **flew away** to find new homes.

Not to mention the poor old **beavers** that needed the roots and branches of the riverbank **willow trees** to build their **dams.** Without dams to **hold** the gushing river back, the beavers' **homes** were **washed away.**

Before long, it was clear that removing the **wolves** had had a devastating **knock-on effect** on the whole **ecosystem** of the park. Once people **figured** out what was **going on,** wolves were **reintroduced** to the area ... and things quickly began to get **better** again. With the **wolves** back on the scene, eventually the **wilderness,** in all its **natural glory** – along with the **balance** of species in the park – was **restored.**

Perhaps if we can learn from this story and find the right way to **support our BEES** over the next few decades, we'll never need to worry about **running out of honey** again.

Humans have a **big responsibility** to take care of **natural ecosystems** because our actions can have an **enormous impact** on them. This can even lead to some species becoming **endangered**.

Sometimes it's obvious that **human actions** are putting animals **at risk,** like when **gamekeepers** kill **birds of prey** so that they can keep the **pheasants** and **grouse** – which the birds of prey usually **eat** – for **human use**. And when **poachers** hunt **rhinos** for their **horns, elephants** for their **tusks, snakes** for their **skin** and **red foxes** for their **fur**.

But sometimes we don't realise that what we're doing might be **harmful**. Many of the **activities** we carry out, as well as the things that we **eat** and **buy,** require the chopping down of many trees and the pumping out of **greenhouse gases,** destroying the homes and risking the lives of many animals in the process.

Since the 1970s, **human actions** have **reduced** the **populations** of thousands of **vertebrate** species (animals with a **backbone**) by a staggering **60%**. Animal populations aren't just getting **smaller**, some species are **dying out** entirely. We have already lost **400 vertebrate species** over the past 100 years and a further **515** land-based vertebrate species are on the **VERY BRINK** of extinction **RIGHT NOW**. These include the **Sumatran rhino**, the **Española giant tortoise** and many types of **Harlequin frog**.

It is estimated that a staggering **1 MILLION MORE SPECIES** could become extinct, many of them over the next few decades. In fact, scientists **warn** that - unless we make **big changes now** - we are heading towards the Earth's **Sixth Mass Extinction**.

This loss of **wildlife** isn't just something that's happening in countries **far away**. One-quarter of **British mammals** have already been **lost**, and 1 in 4 **species** - including the red squirrel, the wildcat, and the grey long-eared bat - are now at risk of being **wiped out** from the British Isles. Many **British bird species** are under threat too and there has been a **huge decline** in the numbers of **garden favourites**, such as **starlings, sparrows** and **cuckoos**.

It's so **important** that we become **aware** of the **impacts** of our actions, and that we **remember** that us humans are part of **delicately balanced** ecosystems too. Our **VERY LIVES depend** on a wide range of **unsuspecting** creatures – from the tiny **insects** and **worms** that pollinate our **food crops** and look after the **soil** to huge **elephants** and **whales** that help to regulate the levels of **carbon dioxide** in our atmosphere. Not to mention the creatures in our oceans that many people depend on for food. In return, we need to make sure we **protect** and **look after** them all, along with the **habitats** that they call home. But don't worry, it's not too late to **repair** some of the **damage** we've already done to our wildlife. I'll be talking about ways you can **help** with this at the **end** of this book.

But while we rely on all these creatures to help us **grow** the **crops** that we need to eat, one of the only insects that actually **PRODUCES** stuff that is eaten by humans

is the **humble honey bee.** So, before we move on, I'll leave you with just one more **weird use** for that yummy **bee barf** (sorry, I mean **honey**) ...

and that is ... relieving **dry skin.** Yep, honey can help **soothe** dry skin conditions, such as a common type of **dermatitis** that mainly affects the **scalp.** If you've got a **dry** and **itchy** scalp, which probably means you are also rather prone to **dandruff,** rubbing a bit of **diluted honey** on your head (as long as you are not **allergic** to it) and leaving it for a **few hours** might actually **help.** But did you know that there's another even **weirder** thing that you can do to cure **dandruff?**

WHAT MIGHT BE AN EFFECTIVE CURE FOR DANDRUFF?

A BOILING A BEETROOT AND MASSAGING IT INTO YOUR SCALP EVERY NIGHT

B SLEEPING WITH A CAT ON YOUR HEAD

C EATING A COCONUT EVERY DAY

D WASHING YOUR HAIR WITH GARLIC BUTTER

Did you know that although human hair is pretty **bendy,** it is actually incredibly **strong?** It may not **feel** it when your little brother tries to pull a **clump** of it out of your head, but, gram for gram, hair is as strong as **aluminium.** It is even as strong as **Kevlar,** which is the stuff used to make **bullet-proof vests.**

Human hair is **so** strong because it is made mainly of the protein **keratin** that also makes up our **skin** and our **nails.** Keratin is composed of tiny **fibres** that are **twisted** round and round each other to form **ropes,** just like a tiny version of the kind of rope you might use to swing on in the **woods,** or use for a **tug-of-war.**

Incredibly, a single human hair can support around **100 g** in weight – that's the weight of 2 small **chocolate bars.** That's quite a heavy load for a **solitary hair.** If you were to consider that a whole **head** of hair contains up to **150,000** strands of hair, **in theory** your mop could support a mega **15,000 kg** hanging off it. That's about the weight of **2 elephants.** Imagine them **swinging** on yer noggin!

It would probably be best to twist your hair into a **plait** before trying this at home, so all the individual hairs can **work together** and take an **equal share** of the weight. And it may be a good idea to try out picking up your **little sister** before you attempt to lift an **elephant.** And I can't promise it won't **hurt.** On second thoughts, maybe just take my word for it. After all, we all know that **Rapunzel** managed the weight of her Prince ...

One of the **problems** with hair is that it can get pretty **greasy,** and your **scalp** underneath it can get quite **dry** and **itchy** and **flaky,** leaving little **white flecks** of **skin** on the shoulders of your **school jumper.** This is what's known as **dandruff.** Dandruff can also be caused by skin conditions such as **eczema,** or by the overgrowth of a type of **fungus** on your scalp. It may sound **gross,** but this fungus is actually pretty **common.**

Whatever the cause, **preventing** dandruff is one of the reasons why some people think it's generally a good idea to **wash** your **hair** and your **head** regularly with products that can help to **moisturise** your scalp. But there's really no need to spend lots of money on **expensive** shampoos and conditioners - **natural** products are often just as **good,** and better for the **environment** too.

I'M GOING TO CHAT TO YOU ABOUT SOME POSSIBLE NATURAL SOLUTIONS TO DANDRUFF, BUT BEFORE I START, IT'S VERY IMPORTANT THAT YOU MAKE SURE YOU DON'T HAVE AN ALLERGY BEFORE TRYING OUT THESE IDEAS.

If you happen to be near a **jungle**, look out for some **wild ginger** bulbs. Simply give them a **squeeze** and the juice acts as a nice moisturising **natural shampoo**. The **oil** from a jungle **coconut** will also do a good job of **moisturising** your scalp and preventing **dandruff**. But I'm afraid it **WON'T** do much if you just **eat** it.

Amazingly, **garlic** can also be useful as it can help **eliminate** those dandruff-causing **fungi**. If you want to **try** this at home, assuming you're not **allergic**, it's probably best to **massage** a small amount of **crushed garlic** into your **scalp**, adding a bit of **honey** to neutralise the **smell**, and then use a good soap or shampoo to **wash it well away.** I wouldn't recommend using **garlic BUTTER** to wash your hair though. Butter is pretty **greasy** so it would be a **nightmare** to try and get it all out.

So what about **sleeping** with a **cat** on your head? Well, I guess this might keep your scalp nice and **warm** at night, which might make it less prone to **drying out** and **flaking,** but it's unlikely to be very **helpful** if you also want a good night's **sleep.** Unless you're only aiming for a **catnap.**

This leaves us with the **strange** possibility that you can use **beetroot** to treat dandruff. Indeed, beetroot is rich in **vitamin C,** which is said to be good for boosting the **immune system** ... and for healthy **skin.** All you have to do is **boil** a beetroot, including the **green bits** at the top. Then, once it's **cool,** chop it up and blend it with some grated fresh **ginger,** along with some gentle natural acid like **lemon juice** or **cider vinegar,** to make a **paste.** Then, simply **rub** the nice beetrooty paste all over your **scalp,** wrap your hair in a **towel** (probably not your mum's best white one) and go to **bed.** In the morning, **wash** the paste off with a **gentle shampoo.**

THE **ANSWER** IS **A**

BOILING A BEETROOT AND MASSAGING IT INTO YOUR SCALP EVERY NIGHT MIGHT BE AN EFFECTIVE CURE FOR DANDRUFF.

Apparently, if you do this for **five nights** in a row you should end up with a lovely **itch-free** scalp and you'll be able to go to school without any **fungus** on your head or annoying **white flakes** on your shoulders. Not that I've **tried** it. I'd be more **concerned** that I might end up with **purple hair.**

That's quite enough about head **fungi.** But speaking of a **fun guy** ... the world record for the **longest** hair was set in the 1940s by a Hindu man, whose hair measured a crazy **7–8 m** in length. His name was **Rapunzo.** No, it wasn't really, that was me being **silly.** And making a **pun-zo.** Sorry, I'm really **embarrassing** myself now. Moving on ...

Anyway, maybe if you tried the same hair-growing **trick** as our friend Rapunzo and then **dangled** your **luscious locks** out of a fourth-floor window, it might be just about **long** enough for a handsome prince or princess to **climb** up it. Although perhaps it's not worth spending a **lifetime** growing your hair on the **off chance** that a **hair-climbing** situation might arise.

By the way, did you know that every **strand** of your hair **grows** about **12 cm** every year? That might not sound **much**, but if you **add** all that new hair together, your head can produce a grand total of about **16 km** of hair every year. That's enough to **wrap** all the way around more than **50 football pitches**. If you don't **cut** it, that is. And if you laid it **end-to-end**. Which is **unlikely** to happen really. But it's a **cool idea**.

Speaking of **cool ideas,** did you know that we're likely to be **eating** some pretty **cool new** things in the future?

WHICH OF THESE ARE WE MOST LIKELY TO BE EATING MORE OF IN THE FUTURE?

MENU

A LAB-GROWN BEEF

B INSECTS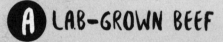

C FOOD FROM BACTERIA

D ALL OF THEM

I know what you're thinking – none of these options sound very **tasty**. And anyway, what is **wrong** with the food we eat at the moment? Well, over the **coming years** we humans are going to have to make some pretty big **changes** to the way we **produce and consume food**.

The **population** of the world is **growing** by an unbelievable **70 million** people every year – that's more than the **entire** population of the **UK**. In order to feed all those **hungry mouths**, by the year **2050** it's predicted that we will need to be producing **twice as much** food as we do today.

But we can't just keep doing **more** of what we're **already doing**. In fact, we should really be doing **LESS**. Today's practices of **industrial food production** – from growing crops using **intensive farming** practices to **transport** and **packaging** – produce more than **one-third** of all greenhouse gas emissions, which, as you know, are having a **huge** impact on our **climate**.

The **extreme weather** events caused by climate change that I mentioned earlier - such as heatwaves, droughts and floods - are actually **REDUCING** our planet's ability to grow and produce **nutritious crops.**

Rising temperatures over the past 30 years have already reduced the **yields** (how much they produce) of all major global **cereal crops,** such as **rice** and **wheat,** whilst some **wild varieties** of other **yummy** foods - such as chocolate, coffee and avocados - are now threatened to the point of **extinction.** It is predicted that by **2050,** the risk of extreme weather events hitting several major **food-producing regions** of the world **AT THE SAME TIME** could more than triple, which would be **disastrous** for global food production.

In other words, not only do modern **intensive farming** practices **damage our planet,** but they are now producing **LESS AND LESS** nutritious food. Clearly, we're going to have to do things **a bit differently** from now on if we're going to **feed** the world's growing population. And believe-it-or-not, some of the **weird-sounding** food alternatives in this question could be the **answer ...**

To work out **which**, we first need to understand exactly **WHY** modern farming is having such a **negative impact** on our planet.

Firstly, **intensive farming** often requires huge numbers of **trees** to be cut down to **clear land** for crops, releasing lots of heat-trapping carbon dioxide back into the atmosphere. In fact, **intensive farming** is by far the biggest cause of **global deforestation**.

This also brings more **wild animals** into **contact** with humans, increasing the chance of a **new disease** being passed to humans.

Intensive farming also uses lots of **chemical fertilisers** that release **nitrous oxide**, as well as **pesticides** that can cause **pollution** and **kill insects**. Lastly, intensive farming severely **damages our soil**. And, although soil might not **look** like much, it is **HUGELY** important.

The **uppermost** layer of soil is known as **topsoil,** and it is high in **nutrients** and **organic matter** (dead plants and animals). It can take a whopping **500 years** to form just **2.5 cm** of this **yummy brown** stuff.

Healthy topsoil is **crucial** for the production of **nutritious crops,** like fruit and vegetables and those that make bread and breakfast cereals. In fact, more than 95% of what we **eat** is **dependent** on healthy soil. Yet, over the past 150 years, **intensive farming** practices – along with **deforestation,** more **extreme rainfall** (that washes topsoil away into **rivers)** and **drying** due to climate change – have led to **around a third** of our planet's juicy topsoil being **damaged** or **destroyed.** This has led to a **reduction** both in the **yields of crops** and in how **nutritious** they are. Today, topsoil across the globe is being lost **10–100 times faster** than it can be made, and some experts have even said we could have just **60 years** of harvests left. **Eek!**

Another problem with farming practices that **damage our soil** is that this not only makes it harder to **grow crops,** but it also **increases the greenhouse effect.** You see, healthy soil (including **peat soil** which I'll come back to in a minute) **stores** a gigantic **70%** of our planet's **land-based carbon.**

> OH NO! DOES THAT MEAN NO MORE CARROTS?!

HOW COME?

Well, topsoil is full of **tiny creatures**, such as **earthworms**, **bacteria** and **fungi** that help to **release the carbon** from dead plants and animals and **incorporate it** into the **soil**. This is a crucial process for keeping our topsoil **healthy**. For example, earthworms **wiggle** and **burrow** into the earth, creating little holes that **loosen** the soil and let **air** and **water** in.

But the problem is, when soil is **repeatedly ploughed** during **intensive farming**, many of the **carbon-containing** plant-root systems are damaged. In addition, repeated ploughing alters the **balance** of the creatures living in the soil: many of the fungi and earthworms **are killed**, whilst the numbers of certain types of bacteria **increase**. These bacteria then start to **feed off** the **carbon** that has been **stored** in the soil for **centuries**, releasing **big quantities** of it back into the atmosphere as **carbon dioxide**. All this extra carbon dioxide adds to our **fluffy blanket**, increasing **global warming**.

> WE HAVE NOW LOST AROUND 80% OF OUR EARTHWORMS, WHICH MEANS THAT WE CAN NO LONGER RELY ON THEM TO REPLENISH HEALTHY SOIL.

To make matters **worse**, if **livestock** or heavy **farm machinery trample** on the soil, the soil gets **compacted** (squashed) and is **even less** able to **hold onto** its stored carbon, so even more of it is released back into the atmosphere. Compacted soil also **holds less water,** meaning plants growing in it struggle to get the **water** and **nutrients** they need.

But it's not just about **how we use** the land we farm on, it's also about what **other land** gets damaged in the process. So let's talk for a minute about **peat bogs.** Peat bogs are a type of **wetland** found in almost every country on Earth. **Wetlands** such as peat bogs are incredibly **important** as they help to **protect us** from floods and storms. Which is why it's so worrying that **more than half** of our wetlands have been lost in the past **100 years** due to a combination of **natural factors** (made worse by climate change) and **human activities** such as **agriculture** and **building works.**

Peat bogs are **particularly** important as they contain **peat soil,** which is the largest **natural carbon store** on our planet. In fact, peat soils store **twice as much** carbon as all the world's **forests.** But our precious peat bogs are **drying out** – as a result of climate change, being drained to clear land for farming, or being **dug up** to be used as **garden soils.** And this is resulting in **LOTS** of **stored carbon** being **released** back into the atmosphere.

One thing is **totally clear** then: we need to **urgently change** how we are **using the land** and **treating the soils** on our planet. If we look after them better, our soils could continue to **store carbon,** reducing global warming, and could produce more of the **nutritious crops** that we'll need to feed the world's **growing population.** Double whammy.

Does this give you any **clues** as to what the **answer** to the **question** might be? Which foods of the future might make **better use** of our land? Or perhaps use **no land at all?** Do you think it would be better for our **soils** if we made **beef in a lab,** produced food from **bacteria** or **ate more insects?**

Hold on, before we explore any of those **strange-sounding ideas,** does all this mean we should be **doing away** with farming **ENTIRELY?!**

No, not at all. You see, it's not the fact that we're **farming** that's the problem, it's **HOW** we're farming. And the **good news** is that there are now lots of farmers and scientists out there who are developing **far less-damaging alternatives** to intensive farming techniques.

For example, most intensive farming uses **monoculture,** which means planting **only one type** of crop – kinda like how a **monobrow** is only one eyebrow. With monoculture, farmers can use **machines** to plant and look after the crops, which means they can be planted **faster.** But monoculture is really not a very good **use of land.** Plus, it's terrible in terms of **protecting wildlife.** And, as we know, **heavy machinery** damages the soil and pumps out **greenhouse gases.**

So **scientists** are exploring the possibility of **replacing** heavy tractors with **small mobile robot tractors** that could do the same job **without** compacting the soil. These **mini tractors** could be used to spray water or pesticides on **individual plants** that need them rather than the **whole field** – causing **less harm** to **pollinating insects** such as bees and allowing the whole system to be more **efficient.**

An **EVEN BETTER** alternative that's being explored by some farmers is **replacing** monoculture entirely and using 'double-cropping' instead. In double-cropping, **two** different types of plants that **complement** each other are grown in the **same field.** No, not ones that tell each other they **look pretty today,** that's a **compliment;** I mean ones that grow **even better** when they're together. For example, small plants that need a lot of **shade** can be grown underneath **big leafy** ones. This **sneaky** technique increases the **amount of food** that can be produced in a **field,** without needing any more **land.**

Another technique is to incorporate **trees** onto farms or pastures. Known as **agroforestry,** this helps to **regenerate damaged soils.** Agroforestry can even improve the **yields** of crops.

But what about the damage done to the environment by the use of **chemical fertilisers?** Well, **ORGANIC** farming techniques make use of **animal waste** (manure) or other plant products as **natural fertilisers.** The only problem is, this often results in crops producing **smaller yields.**

Some **eco-conscious** farmers have even started to grow 'food forests'. To make a food forest, a **huge variety** of edible plants and trees are planted in one area, just like what you might find in a **natural ecosystem** like a rainforest – except in food forests, everything is **edible!**

As well as taking up **far less land,** growing a **variety** of plants **alongside** one another means that a **large range of insects** can flourish too. Not only does this help **restore wildlife,** but the **different** insects also keep each other's **numbers** at bay, so there's less chance that one **pesky species** will just **take over** and **eat** all the crops. And that means that fewer **chemical pesticides** are needed.

Food forests may take a bit more **time** to set up than traditional **monoculture** (as crops need to be planted **by hand**), but this also means less soil-compacting, fossil-fuel-guzzling **heavy machinery. Hurray!** And once all the crops are **planted,** the **food forest** requires virtually **no attention** and **no fertilisers,** as the ecosystem simply looks after **itself.**

Techniques like these that **look after the land,** use less **heavy machinery** and require **fewer chemicals** are known as **regenerative farming.** If more farmers used such techniques to **grow good quality nutritious crops** it would not only have a huge impact on our **global greenhouse gas emissions,** but would also help to **restore** our **soils** and our **wildlife.** Hopefully we'll be seeing **more and more** of these techniques being used in the **future.**

Whilst **these techniques** certainly provide farmers with more **sustainable** ways to grow **crops** in the future, if we really want to be able to **feed the world** whilst also **looking after** the planet, we also need to take a **close look** at the way we're **farming animals.**

Today, a staggering **four-fifths** of the world's precious **farmlands** are being used for **livestock** – that's animals bred for meat, eggs and milk. Farming livestock not only results in **compacting** of the soil, but also in huge amounts of **methane** being produced in the **burps** of cows and sheep and lots of **nitrous oxide** being emitted from animal waste.

MYSELF AND THE OTHER 1.5 BILLION COWS ON OUR PLANET BURP AND FART MORE THAN 680 BILLION LITRES OF METHANE EVERY DAY.

PARP!

PARP!

Plus, the **HUGE** areas of land that have to be cleared to give these animals space to graze leads to – you guessed it – more **deforestation**. And it's not just the land needed for **grazing** the **animals** that's a problem: currently **one-third** of the world's **croplands** are being used to **grow food** to **feed** these animals.

But here's the **CRAZY** thing. Despite taking up masses of farmland, livestock only provide us with **less than one-fifth** of the **calories** that the world's population **eat** and only about **one-third** of the **protein**. What this means is that **farming animals** is a very **inefficient** way of using our planet's **limited land** and **resources** to feed us all. All in all, growing **more crops** in a more **sustainable** way – and feeding them **directly** to humans – would be a **far better** idea.

BURP!

BURP!

PARDON ME!

DEFORESTATION, COW AND SHEEP BURPS, AND FERTILISERS PRODUCE MORE GREENHOUSE GASES THAN ALL THE WORLD'S CARS, LORRIES AND PLANES PUT TOGETHER.

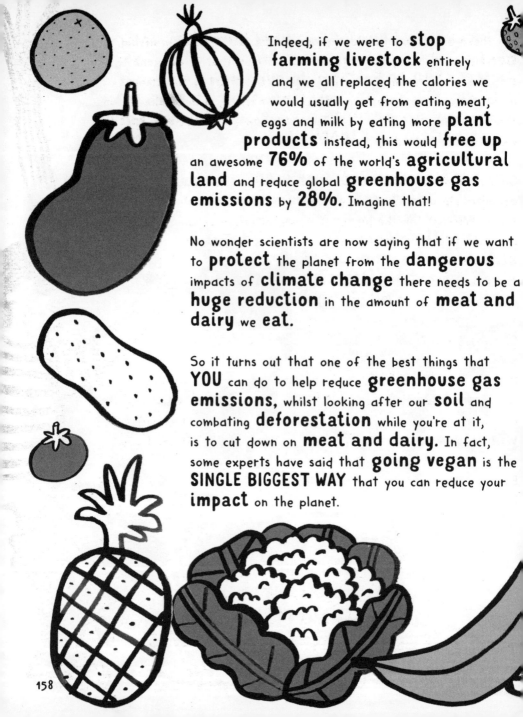

Indeed, if we were to **stop farming livestock** entirely and we all replaced the calories we would usually get from eating meat, eggs and milk by eating more **plant products** instead, this would **free up** an awesome **76%** of the world's **agricultural land** and reduce global **greenhouse gas emissions** by **28%**. Imagine that!

No wonder scientists are now saying that if we want to **protect** the planet from the **dangerous** impacts of **climate change** there needs to be a **huge reduction** in the amount of **meat and dairy** we **eat**.

So it turns out that one of the best things that **YOU** can do to help reduce **greenhouse gas emissions**, whilst looking after our **soil** and combating **deforestation** while you're at it, is to cut down on **meat and dairy**. In fact, some experts have said that **going vegan** is the **SINGLE BIGGEST WAY** that you can reduce your **impact** on the planet.

For those of you partial to the odd **beef burger**, I'm afraid that **beef** is particularly bad. Studies have shown that if we want to help stop the planet from **heating up even more,** the amount of **beef** eaten by people in **wealthy** nations, such as the UK and the US, needs to fall by **90%** and the amount of **cows' milk** we drink needs to drop by **60%.**

Sadly, choosing **grass-fed** or **organic** varieties of beef **doesn't** actually help much. In fact, in some ways they can actually make things **worse** for the planet. You see, although organic farming does use **fewer chemicals** and grass-fed cows do **store more carbon** in the **soil,** allowing cows to **roam freely** (which is certainly **kinder** to the cows) requires **FAR MORE LAND.**

So, if you really like the **taste** or **texture** of meat but are worried about the **impact** on the planet, it might be a **good idea** to start trying out some of the tasty **meat alternatives** that are now available in the shops. Maybe see if you and your family can have at least **one day a week** where you eat only **vegan** or **vegetarian** food.

But enough about what we might be eating **LESS** of in the future. Let's get back to what foods we might be eating **MORE** of ...

Given everything we've just talked about, it would **make sense** that the absolute **LAST** thing we should be eating **MORE OF** in the future is **beef**, right? **Not necessarily ...**

If you simply can't **resist** a real-deal **beef burger,** fear not. You will be **relieved** to know that scientists are now working on ways to grow **real beef** in huge quantities ... in a **laboratory.** This may sound a bit icky, but **lab-grown beef** looks, smells and tastes exactly the same as **real beef.** And the **best news** is that one day this kind of **beef** could be made in a way that emits virtually no **greenhouse gases** and uses virtually no **land.** And the people **making it** wouldn't even have to **kill** any animals. All they'd need is some **cells** from a cow.

However, before you go dashing off to try and **sink your teeth** into a **lab-grown beef burger,** it's worth noting that the first burger to be grown in this way in 2013 cost around **£200,000** to make. So I wouldn't go **nagging** your parents for one **quite yet.** But do keep an **eye out** for all sorts of **'cultured meat'** arriving in your **local supermarket** soon. Scientists predict that **within a few years** cultured beef could be **cheaper** than traditionally grown beef and **far better** for the planet. It may even be **healthier,** as the lab-grown meat can be **engineered** to contain fewer **unhealthy** chemicals, such as **saturated fats.**

So it turns out that, although it's **super-important** that we try to cut down on beef **for now,** in the future we may actually be eating even **MORE** of the stuff than we do today.

Aside from eating **lab-grown beef,** what other **strange** things might we be doing in the **future** to feed the world's growing population?

Well, you might be **surprised** to hear that, whilst the declining numbers of **pollinating insects** are likely to lead to **reductions** in crop yields in the future, **insects** could also be the ANSWER to our food issues. But not through **pollination**. Through **farming** the insects **themselves** and EATING THEM.

WHAT???!!!

Eating insects may sound **revolting** to some, but currently around **2 billion** people on the planet **regularly** eat insects as part of their **normal diet.** The most commonly eaten **critters** are beetles, caterpillars, bees, wasps and ants. But that doesn't take into account the 400 or so 'bug bits' that **you** probably eat on a **daily basis** without even **realising.** Believe it or not, it's totally **normal** to find bits of **mealworms, maggots** or **cockroaches** in everyday foods like chocolate, coffee beans and wheat flour.

EWWW.

But don't worry, these little bug bits are **so small** that you're unlikely to have ever **noticed** them. And even if you **did**, contrary to what you might **imagine**, insects are actually rather **tasty. Termites** are said to have a pleasant **minty** flavour, while **tree worms** taste a bit like **pork rind. Stinkbugs**, on the other hand, may **smell revolting** but, apparently, they taste like **apples. **Not that I've ever **tried one.**

163

Insects are also surprisingly **nutritious.** Most insects contain **similar amounts** of fat, protein, vitamins, fibre and minerals as fish or even **beef.** Some even contain **a lot more.** Indeed, lowly **termites** have **twice as much protein** as beef, whilst some **locusts** and **caterpillars** contain up to **5 times** as much **iron** as the equivalent amount of juicy **cow-flesh.**

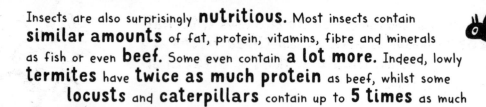

Because insects are **cold-blooded,** they don't waste any of the **energy** they get from their food in **keeping warm.** This makes insects far better at **converting** their food into **body mass** for us to eat than, say, a **nice warm cow.**

Plus, more of an insect's **body mass** is actually **edible** compared to the body mass of a cow. You can pop pretty much an **entire cricket** into your mouth and simply **crunch** it up and only about a **fifth** of it would come out the **other end.** Imagine trying that with a **cow!** Even if you could **FIT** an entire cow into your **mouth,** you'd struggle swallowing down its **bones.**

And, although you can eat **some** of a cow's **internal organs** (known as **offal**), about **three-fifths** of a cow's body is totally **inedible**. That's an **offal** lot of wasted body mass.

Overall this means insects need to be **fed** around **8 times less food** than cows do in order to provide **YOU** with the **same amount** of nutritious calories. Cool, huh? Plus, insects can be fed stuff that isn't otherwise **useful** to us, such as **animal waste** or **inedible plants.**

YOU CAN EAT ALL OF ME!

Most importantly, farming insects is **MUCH** better for the **environment** than farming cows. Not only do they require far less **land-hogging crops** to be grown to feed them, but insects have a much **shorter life cycle** than cows, so they can be grown very **quickly** and farmed in **enormous** quantities on **small areas of land.**

Not to mention the fact that **insect farms** produce a **fraction** of the greenhouse gas emissions that **cattle farms** do, as insects don't require **fertilisers,** they don't produce much **waste,** and insects don't burp or fart out **methane.** (With the notable exception of **termites,** but that's another story). Insect farms could even provide **jobs** for people living in **poor areas.**

Whichever way you look at it, insect farming would give us a highly **sustainable** way of **making food** for humans. So, in the future perhaps we'll all be eating **beetle burgers.** Tasty!

But there's one other **futuristic way** that we might be **making food** in years to come. A method that **cuts out** plants and animals **entirely** and uses some of the most **easy-to-come-by** creatures on Earth instead – **bacteria**.

Scientists in **Finland** are currently working on a simple technique that uses **air, water** and **bacteria** from the **soil**, together with a **small jolt of electricity** (that can be supplied from **renewable** energy sources like **solar power**), to produce a magical **flour-like powder** that they call 'electric protein'.

This **electric protein powder** is packed full of **edible calories** and it can be **shaped** and **moulded** into all sorts of different types of **food**. Not only does it contain **6 times more protein** than traditional **wheat flour,** but making it requires **virtually no land** ... and emits **virtually no greenhouse gases.** How amazing is that?!

The Finnish scientists reckon that in the **future,** electric protein **factories** could be producing enough protein to **feed the world** in an area just the size of **Ohio.**

THE **ANSWER** is **D** IN THE FUTURE WE'RE LIKELY TO BE EATING MORE LAB-GROWN BEEF, INSECTS AND FOOD FROM BACTERIA.

Scientists across the globe are **working hard** to come up with **other** new ways to feed us all. If **exciting new projects** like the one in Finland work out, they could completely **transform** the food industry.

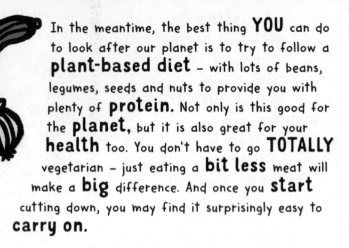

In the meantime, the best thing **YOU** can do to look after our planet is to try to follow a **plant-based diet** – with lots of beans, legumes, seeds and nuts to provide you with plenty of **protein.** Not only is this good for the **planet,** but it is also great for your **health** too. You don't have to go **TOTALLY** vegetarian – just eating a **bit less** meat will make a **big** difference. And once you **start** cutting down, you may find it surprisingly easy to **carry on.**

Another way you can **help** is by **cutting down** on the amount of food you **waste.** Every year, a shocking **one-third** of the world's food is wasted. If we all only bought what we actually **needed** we could go a long way towards solving the world's **food problems** and reducing **global warming.**

Wasting less food might not only mean **buying** less stuff that's going to **go off** before you get a chance to eat it, but also **choosing** more fruit and vegetables that look **weird** or **ugly.** You know, the **sad and lonely** ones in the supermarket aisles that nobody wants, but that **taste** just as **good.** Strange-looking knobbly carrots, bulging peppers, bendy cucumbers or double-headed potatoes. There are now even **companies** that specialise in selling 'ugly produce' and excess food that restaurants and cafes are getting rid of at the end of a day. They usually **charge you** a lot less for it too, so **everybody wins.**

Other than **wasting** less food, you can also help protect the planet by looking out for fruit and vegetables that have been produced through **sustainable** or **organic** farming methods. And you can try to buy food that's been grown **locally,** reducing the carbon emissions from **fossil-fuel-guzzling** lorries and planes that are needed to **transport** food from **other countries.**

You can find more tips on this at the end of this book. But if you want to live in a **REALLY REALLY** sustainable way, you could start **growing your own** fruit and vegetables. Lots of people are doing this now, and it is **great fun** too. All you'll need is a little patch of **healthy soil** (even just a **window box** will do), some **sunlight** and a sprinkle of **rain.**

Speaking of rain, did you know that there's a strange **planet** on which it might **rain diamonds?**

ON WHICH PLANET(S) MIGHT IT RAIN DIAMONDS?

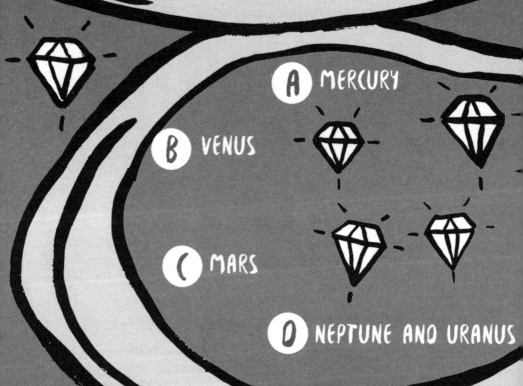

A MERCURY

B VENUS

C MARS

D NEPTUNE AND URANUS

Wouldn't it be nice if **jewels** simply fell from the **sky**? Well, somewhere in our **solar system,** they do.

In order for **rain** to occur – or indeed for any type of **weather** to occur – a planet needs to have a **layer of air circling** around it that can **flow** in **different directions.** This airflow carries **heat** and **water vapour** around the planet, giving rise to wind, clouds, rain and storms. We call this layer of air around a planet its **atmosphere** and it is made of **gases** that are held in place by the force of **gravity.** Otherwise, they'd just **fly out** into **space** as the planet **spins** on its axis, like a **pile of dust** on a **merry-go-round.**

On Earth, our **atmosphere** consists of around **78%** **nitrogen** and **21% oxygen,** with small amounts of **argon** and other gases such as **carbon dioxide** and **water vapour,** as well as **tiny particles** such as dust, smoke and pollen. The atmosphere **extends** out from the surface of the Earth for **hundreds of km,** getting **thinner and thinner** until it gradually fades away into **space.** This means that the air pressure gets **lower** the **further** from Earth you go.

You might **notice** this **thinning out** of the atmosphere if you were an **explorer** climbing a **mountain.** The **higher** you climb, the **lower** the **air pressure** would get. When the air pressure is lower, it becomes harder to get enough **oxygen** into your lungs, so you might feel a bit **breathless.** Even if you are just **sitting still.** That's why **extra oxygen** is pumped into the cabins of **aeroplanes,** so that you can breathe **normally** even though you're **high up** in the sky where the air pressure is **very low.**

It's probably best **not to fly** anywhere these days if you can possibly help it though. Whilst **many** forms of **transport** burn **fossil fuels** and therefore **emit carbon dioxide**, aeroplanes **emit the most by far.** For example, for a **family of 4** traveling from **London** to **Rome**, going by **plane** produces **4 times more** carbon dioxide than doing the **same** journey by **car**, **3 times more** than travelling by **national rail** (as those trains often still run off **diesel**) and a whopping **22 times more** than travelling by **international rail**. That's because international trains are mostly **electric** and **electricity** can be produced using **renewable** energy sources such as **wind, hydroelectric dams** or **solar power** – or by **nuclear** power – all of which emit little or no **carbon dioxide.**

DID YOU KNOW THAT RETURN TRANSATLANTIC FLIGHTS FOR A FAMILY OF 4 FROM THE UK EMIT THE SAME AMOUNT OF CARBON DIOXIDE AS AN AVERAGE HOUSEHOLD'S ELECTRICITY OVER 13 YEARS?

Anyway, back to the Earth's **atmosphere** ... Our atmosphere is divided into **4 layers,** a bit like the layers of an **onion.**

You can find most of the Earth's **air molecules** within the **first** layer, called the **troposphere.** This **dense** layer extends about **10 km** from the Earth's surface and is where most of our **weather** occurs.

The next layer of much **thinner** air is called the **stratosphere,** which extends for about another **30 km** or so.

THE THERMOSPHERE IS WHERE THE BEAUTIFUL AURORA BOREALIS OCCURS, OTHERWISE KNOWN AS THE NORTHERN LIGHTS.

Then there's about **70 km** of **mesosphere**.

And finally, there's the **thermosphere** that extends to the edge of **space**.

Given that a planet needs to have an **atmosphere** in order to produce **rain** – even the **sparkly diamond** variety – this rules out poor old **Mercury.** You see, Mercury has only about **one-tenth** of the **mass** of Earth, which means that the **force of gravity** pulling its **atmospheric gases** towards it is **far less** than that on Earth. As a result, most of the **gases** released from Mercury's surface can **escape** its gravitational pull and **shoot** out into **space,** leaving Mercury with virtually **no atmosphere.**

Mercury's **lack of atmosphere** not only means that there's **no weather,** it also means that Mercury has enormous **variations in temperature** between day and night.

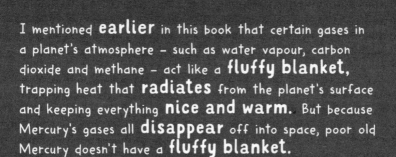

I mentioned **earlier** in this book that certain gases in a planet's atmosphere – such as water vapour, carbon dioxide and methane – act like a **fluffy blanket,** trapping heat that **radiates** from the planet's surface and keeping everything **nice and warm.** But because Mercury's gases all **disappear** off into space, poor old Mercury doesn't have a **fluffy blanket.**

Now, Mercury is much **closer** to the Sun than Earth, which means that when the surface of Mercury is **facing** the Sun (during the **day**) it can reach **super-high** temperatures of more than **420°C.** However, when the Sun goes **down** at night, with no nice **warm blanket** of greenhouse gases to prevent the heat from **escaping** back out to **space,** the surface of Mercury can **drop** to a terrible **-170°C.** No wonder no one lives there!

But what about the **other** planets that **DO** have an atmosphere? Take **Venus,** for example.

Venus has a similar **density** to Earth, so it has a similar **force of gravity** pulling gases towards its surface. This means, just like on Earth, gases remain trapped in layers around the planet forming an **atmosphere.** However, Venus' atmosphere is far **denser** than that on Earth.

Now Venus **ought to be** a lot **cooler** than Mercury because it's **further** from the Sun. In fact, like Earth, Venus is in the Sun's 'habitable zone'.

What's a **habitable zone,** I hear you cry? Well, it's an area around a **star** where planets are, **in theory,** just the right temperature for **water** to exist on them in its **liquid form.** In this zone, planets are far enough away from the **flaming ball of gas** that water on their surface shouldn't **boil away,** but close enough that it shouldn't **freeze.** This **ought to** give a planet the perfect **conditions** to sustain **life.** As **Goldilocks** would say, "Not too hot, not too cold. **Just right.**" And actually, a star's habitable zone is sometimes known as the **Goldilocks Zone.**

Goldy

Bears 3

I say 'in theory', as while Venus' surface **SHOULD** be cool enough for life to appear, Venus not only has a **super-dense** atmosphere, but a **whopping 97%** of it is **carbon dioxide** (along with tiny amounts of nitrogen, sulphur dioxide and water vapour). This means that Venus has the **strongest greenhouse effect** of any planet in our solar system. As a result, almost **ALL** the **heat** that radiates from Venus's surface is **trapped** by its atmosphere, stopping the poor planet from being able to **cool down.** And the **hotter** the surface gets, the **faster** it heats up. So Venus is like an **oven,** heating up so much that it ends up **even hotter** than Mercury. At a roasting **462°C,** it's hot enough there to **melt lead.** So, while Venus **OUGHT** to be habitable, its dense atmosphere makes it **so hot** that there's no chance of any life-sustaining **liquid water** I'm afraid.

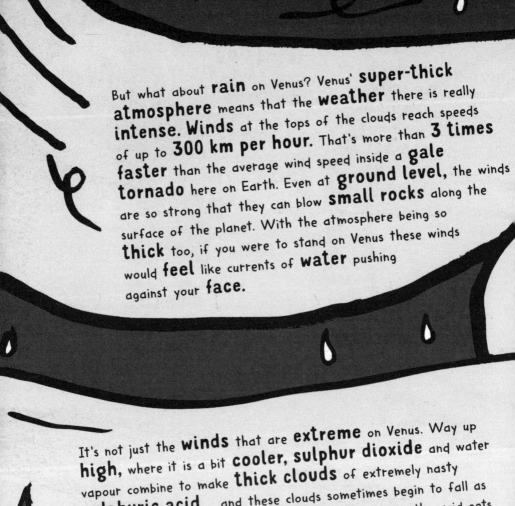

But what about **rain** on Venus? Venus' **super-thick atmosphere** means that the **weather** there is really **intense. Winds** at the tops of the clouds reach speeds of up to **300 km per hour.** That's more than **3 times faster** than the average wind speed inside a **gale tornado** here on Earth. Even at **ground level,** the winds are so strong that they can blow **small rocks** along the surface of the planet. With the atmosphere being so **thick** too, if you were to stand on Venus these winds would **feel** like currents of **water** pushing against your **face.**

It's not just the **winds** that are **extreme** on Venus. Way up **high,** where it is a bit **cooler, sulphur dioxide** and water vapour combine to make **thick clouds** of extremely nasty **sulphuric acid** ... and these clouds sometimes begin to fall as **acid rain.** Although, it's **so hot** that as soon as the acid gets close to Venus's surface, it just **evaporates** again.

Good thing too, because this **acidic** rain would be **highly corrosive**. Even the **teeny tiny** amounts of **very dilute** sulphuric acid found in **acid rain** here on Earth – formed due to **sulphur dioxide** from factory **waste gases** dissolving in water droplets in the air – is enough to **kill insects** and **fish, damage trees**, cause **paint to peel**, corrode steel bridges, **weather** statues and stone buildings and **damage** our **health**.

Imagine what being caught in an **acid rainstorm** on Venus could do to you! No wonder Venus is sometimes known as **Earth's evil twin** ...

OK, so if Mercury has **no** rain and Venus has hellish **acidic** rain, what about the next planet out from the Sun, **Mars?** Any **diamond rain** there?

Mars is often called the **Red Planet** due to the reddish **iron oxide** rust—like **dust** that covers its surface. Like Venus and Earth, Mars also sits in the Sun's **habitable zone.** However, just like Mercury, its mass is only **one-tenth** of the mass of the Earth, so it has much **less gravity** to create an atmosphere. Mars certainly has a **bit** more atmosphere than **naked** Mercury, but not **enough** to trap very much **heat** at all. This means that on Mars it's **far too cold** at night to be able to sustain life.

However, there is **just enough** atmosphere on Mars to create some types of **weather.** Winds can **whip** up the surface into some of the largest **dust storms** in the galaxy and when the temperature drops at night occasional **turbulent storms** can even result in **snow!** Snow on Mars might **sound** pretty cool, but that's not the **diamond rain** we're searching for.

So that leaves us with **Neptune** and **Uranus**. Both Neptune and Uranus have a **mass** more than **15 times** that of Earth, meaning they have far more gravity to **pull** their atmosphere in, making the **air pressure** at their surface **millions** of times **more intense** than on Earth. In you **stood** on the surface (not that you could) you'd be **crushed to death** by the atmosphere.

These planets are both surrounded by **liquid** and **gas** that is rich in molecules called **hydrocarbons**. Hydrocarbons are made up of **hydrogen** and **carbon** atoms and are the main component of **fossil fuels** such as coal and oil.

When **hydrocarbons** are subjected to **huge** amounts of **heat** and **pressure**, the carbon and hydrogen atoms can **split apart** from each other. The high pressure can then cause the **carbon** atoms to **squeeze** tightly together to form **crystals** of ... yep, you guessed it. **Diamond.**

You see, just like **coal**, diamond is simply made of plain old **carbon**. It's just that, in **diamond**, the carbon atoms are **joined together** in a different way. In fact, if you place **ANY carbon-rich** material at a high enough **pressure**, you could get the carbon atoms in it to **separate** and then come back together to form **diamond**. Scientists have even managed to do this with ... **peanut butter!** For real.

This is exactly what scientists think happens in the **liquid layers** of Neptune and Uranus. The **super-high** pressure causes some of the **hydrocarbons** to split apart and the carbon atoms to come back together again to form tiny **diamonds.** The diamonds slowly **sink like rain** until they reach the **solid surface** of the planet, where they **clump** together to form a beautiful **glittery layer.**

THE ANSWER is 0
iT MiGHT RAiN DiAMONDS ON NEPTUNE AND URANUS.

Diamonds have a **crystal** structure and this not only makes them **super-twinkly** but also **very hard.** You might already know that diamond is the **hardest** naturally-occurring substance on Earth. Diamonds are **so hard** that they are sometimes used as the **tips** of **power drills.**

WHAT YOU MIGHT NOT KNOW THOUGH, IS THAT THERE IS A SUBSTANCE THAT'S EVEN HARDER THAN DIAMOND. YEP. IT'S CALLED LONSDALEITE AND IT COMES FROM METEORITES. YOU CAN USE THAT FACT TO AMAZE YOUR FRIENDS.

Neptune and Uranus are not the **only** planets on which you might find diamonds. There is also an **exoplanet** outside of our solar system called **55 Cancri e** – about twice the size of Earth and 40 light years away – that is affectionately known as the **diamond planet.** Scientists suspect that up to **one-**

third of this planet could be made of **carbon**. Not only that, but it is **so close** to the **star** that it orbits (known as its **parent star**) that it only takes a measly **18 hours** to travel around it – compared to the 365-and-a-quarter days that it takes for the Earth to orbit our parent star, the **Sun**. This means that the **surface temperature** on this diamond planet is a sizzling **2,700°C**. Plus, its **mass** is 8 times greater than that of Earth, making it **more dense** and therefore giving it more **gravity**, so the **air pressure** at its surface could also be **very high**. It is therefore quite **possible** that the temperatures and pressures are high enough to cause the **entire** carbon-rich planet to be **covered in diamonds**.

It has been estimated that all the diamonds on this **glittery** planet would be worth **27 nonillion dollars**. That's 27 with 30 zeros after it!

But diamonds are not the only **crazy** things that you might find **falling as rain** on distant planets ...

WHICH OF THESE ARE YOU LEAST LIKELY TO FIND FALLING AS RAIN ON A FAR-OFF PLANET?

A RUBIES AND SAPPHIRES

B PIECES OF CORK

C ROCKS AND PEBBLES

D SHARDS OF GLASS

If you were to travel through space at the **speed of light** for about 1,000 years, you might happen upon a **Jupiter-like exoplanet** that's about **16 times larger** than Earth, with the catchy name ... HAT-P-7b. This **super-sized** planet (possibly known as **Hattie** to its friends) is **so close** to its **parent star,** that it can reach baking temperatures of around **1,900°C.** Hattie is so **massive** that she has a really **dense atmosphere,** giving rise to **violent weather systems** – such as **powerful winds** and **catastrophic storms.** Not a place you'd choose to go for an **intergalactic holiday.**

This crazy planet is **so hot** that **minerals** on its surface are turned to **vapour.** The vapour rises high into the atmosphere, forming **thick clouds,** which are **blown violently** across the sky. Now one such mineral is aluminium oxide, otherwise known as **corundum,** and this happens to be the **same** mineral that produces ... **rubies and sapphires.** So, when the conditions are right, you just might find sparkling **red and blue gemstones** falling as rain.

If you thought Hattie was **hot,** that's **nothing** compared to scorching **COROT-7b,** an **orange dwarf** that is **23 times closer** to its parent star than Mercury is to the Sun. Maybe they should have called it ... **Scorching Carrot.** Scorching Carrot is **so close** to the star it orbits that it is what's known as **'gravitationally locked',** meaning that the **same side** of it always **faces** its star.

Our Moon is also gravitationally locked in its orbit around the Earth, so we are always looking at the **same side** of it. If you don't believe me, take a look at the **night sky** next time there's a **full Moon.** You'll notice that the **smiley face** of the 'Man in the Moon' always looks **the same.** Unless of course you go to **Australia** or another country in the **Southern Hemisphere,** in which case he'll appear **upside down.** But **wherever** you go, you'll **never** see the **'dark side'** (the back) of the Moon.

Anyway, because Scorching Carrot is gravitationally locked, the side that is **always facing** its star is a bright and blistering **2,600°C,** while the **other** side is in **perpetual** freezing darkness – a chilly **-220°C.**

So what about the **weather?** Well, it's hot enough on the star-facing side to **melt rock**, so this side of Scorching Carrot is covered in lakes of **molten lava**. As a result, the atmosphere consists mainly of **vaporised rock minerals** that **condense** high up in the sky to form 'rock clouds' made of tiny particles of **molten rock.** When these clouds hit a patch of **cooler air**, the molten rock condenses into **tiny pebbles,** which **rain down** from the heavens.

But that's not as **weird** as what happens on exoplanet **HD189733b** (let's call him **Hadrian** because, let's face it, that's a bit of a mouthful), a huge **gas giant** that is a mere 63 light years from Earth. Compared to most other exoplanets, that's practically **next door** to us. Not only does Hadrian reach temperatures of 1,000°C, but **high-speed winds** blow at a terrifying **8,600 km per hour** – that's 7 times faster than the **speed of sound!**

As if this wasn't **scary** enough, high in the atmosphere are clouds laced with **silicate particles,** which probably give the planet a **deep blue hue.** Silicate is similar to **silicon dioxide,** which is the main component of **sand.** And you might know that if sand is subjected to **intense heat** and **pressure** – such as that found in a **furnace** or in the atmosphere of a planet like this one – it turns into **glass.** Therefore, when it rains on Hadrian, it probably rains **shards of glass** that are **blown sideways** by the **howling winds.** Ouch. You'd need more than a small **umbrella** to protect yourself from those. Perhaps you could hide behind a wall? **Hadrian's wall?** (Sorry.)

This leaves **pieces of cork** as the only answer that **ISN'T** a real type of rain.

THE **ANSWER** is B

YOU ARE LEAST LIKELY TO FIND PIECES OF CORK FALLING AS RAIN ON A FAR-OFF PLANET.

Whilst it's true that there are no planets where **champagne corks** magically rain down from the sky, there **IS** an exoplanet that's **so light** that it's almost as if it were **MADE** of cork. TrES-4 (let's call her **Teresa**) is the largest exoplanet so far discovered, being **nearly twice** the size of **Jupiter**. However, Teresa has such a **low density** that it is categorised as a 'puffy' planet and it is thought to have the same **density** as **cork**. Imagine seeing that whopper **floating around** in an intergalactic **bathtub!**

Diamond downpours, ruby rain, puddles of pebbles, gleaming glass clouds and floating puffy planets, could it get any **weirder?** Maybe ... Did you know that there's a place in our **solar system** where you might see a **blue sunset?!**

WHERE IN OUR SOLAR SYSTEM MIGHT YOU SEE A BLUE SUNSET?

A VENUS

B MARS

C MERCURY

D THE MOON

Wouldn't it be **beautiful** if you could watch as the evening sun **sank** down towards the **horizon,** turning the sky around it **bright blue?** Well, if you were to visit one **ethereal** place, this is **exactly** what you'd see.

In order to figure out **where** this strange thing might occur, we first need to understand a bit about why the **sky is blue** and why **sunsets are red** here on **Earth.**

You might already know that **visible white light** from the Sun is actually made up of a **spectrum** of different colours, from **red** to **violet.** You've probably seen this spectrum when sunlight is **dispersed** through **raindrops** on a rainy day and the colours **separate** into a beautiful **rainbow.**

When light travels through a **gas**, like air, the light **bounces off** different **particles** in the gas as it passes **through**. This is called **scattering**. What's interesting is that different **colours** of light are **scattered** by different **amounts** depending on the **size** of the **particles** they bump into. Light at the **blue end** of the spectrum is scattered best by **really tiny** particles such as **gas molecules**, whereas light at the **red end** of the spectrum is scattered best by **slightly larger** particles such as **dust**. This effect is known as **Rayleigh scattering**.

The **gas** in the Earth's **atmosphere** consists mostly of **tiny molecules** of **nitrogen** and **oxygen**. This means that every time light from the Sun passes through **our atmosphere**,

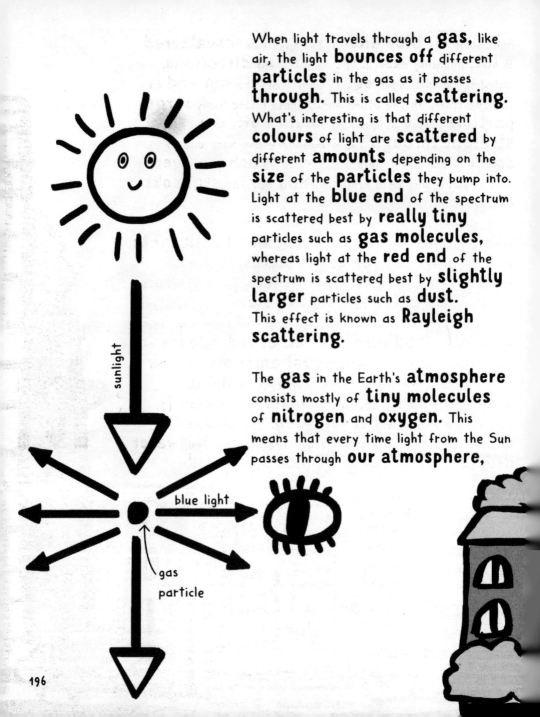

sunlight

blue light

gas particle

light from the **blue end** of the spectrum is **scattered a lot,** bouncing away in lots of different **directions,** including towards your **eyes.** Light from the **red end** of the spectrum, on the other hand, doesn't find many **large particles** (such as dust) to **bounce off,** so it passes **straight through** the atmosphere and back out to **space** – and never gets a chance to **reach** your **eyes.** This explains why on a bright **sunny** day the **sky looks blue.**

In **big cities** the air is full of **chemical pollutants** from things like **car fumes** and **factory smoke,** produced by the burning of **fossil fuels.** These pollutants consist of **particles** that **vary in size,** with each type scattering light from a different part of the spectrum. This means that in **polluted** areas, **all of the colours** of light get scattered by pretty **equal amounts,** meaning that **all the colours** reach your eyes **equally.** Consequently, the sky appears a **mixture** of all colours, making it a boring **white-ish grey.** This explains why **clouds** usually look **white** too – they contain fine **water droplets** that scatter all colours of light **equally.**

OK, SO WHAT ABOUT SUNSETS?

Well, as **evening** approaches, the Sun **dips low** in the sky. This means that it is now a bit **further away** from you compared to when it was **directly overhead** in the **middle** of the day. But more importantly, the Sun's **rays** now have to travel through a lot **more of the atmosphere** before they reach your eyes.

Now here's the **cool** part ... Because the Sun's rays have to travel through **loads more** of the atmosphere, the light at the **blue end** of the spectrum gets scattered **SO MUCH** by the **gazillions** of tiny particles of gas that it **bumps into** on its way to **your eyes** that most of the **blue light** ends up heading **back out to space.** Only the light further towards the **red end** of the spectrum is **left behind,** so this is the only light that actually **finds its way** to you. So, assuming you're somewhere with a nice **unpolluted** sky, the rays from the **setting Sun** will appear as **beautiful reds** and **oranges.**

It is this **same effect** that causes the Moon to **glow red** during a **total lunar eclipse.** Usually the Moon looks **white** because when light from the Sun falls on it **all** the colours of light are **reflected** back to your eyes in **equal amounts.** You can only actually **see** this reflected light at **night,** but it's **always there.** It's just that it is **masked** during the **day** by **brighter** sunlight that reaches your eyes **directly** from the Sun.

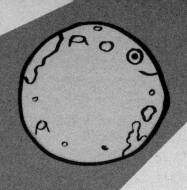

During a **total lunar eclipse** the Earth **lines up exactly** between the Sun and the Moon. This means that the **pesky** Earth gets right **in the way** of the Sun's rays as they try to **shine** onto the Moon. The **only sunlight** that can actually **reach** the Moon are the rays that sneak around the **outside** edges of the Earth – in other words, rays that have passed through the Earth's **atmosphere.** As these rays pass through our **gas-filled** atmosphere, most of the light from the **blue end** of the spectrum is **scattered** away into **space** by the tiny **gas molecules** (just like it does at **sunset**) leaving behind only light from the **red end** of the spectrum to eventually **land** on the **Moon's surface.** From there, the red light is **reflected** back to your **eyes** on Earth ... resulting in a **ghostly red sight** known as a **Blood Moon.** Blood Moons usually occur every **1–2 years.**

BUT HOW DOES ALL THIS HELP US TO FIGURE OUT WHERE WE MIGHT SEE A BLUE SUNSET?

Well, let's start with **Mercury.** The **lack of atmosphere** on this **low-gravity** planet means that if you were to **stand** on its surface (not that you could, you'd **vaporise**) and look up into the **sky**, there would be no **gas molecules** to scatter the Sun's light to you and so virtually **NO** light would reach your **eyes.** Therefore, although it would be **daylight** and you'd be able to see your (vaporised) **body** and everything **around you,** you wouldn't be able to see any colours in the **sky.** Just the **blackness** of **space,** with the Sun and other stars and planets moving across it as **balls of light.** As **night** approached, the Sun would simply **disappear** over the **horizon** and it would get very **suddenly** and completely **dark. No sunsets.**

This is exactly the **same** as what happens on the **Moon.** Although the Moon does have a **very thin** layer of **gases** close to its **surface,** known as the **exosphere,** there are **so few** molecules of **gas** in this layer that it doesn't really scatter much **light.** That's why when you see pictures of **astronauts** on the Moon you can see their **spaceship** but you can't see any **sky.**

At the **opposite extreme,** the tremendously **dense** atmosphere and **thick clouds** on **Venus** stop the Sun's rays from ever **penetrating** through to the **surface** of the planet. No **sunshine** there at all. And certainly no **sunsets.**

moon buggy

203

So what about **Mars?** As I mentioned earlier, the atmosphere on Mars is pretty **thin.** Whilst there are **SOME** small molecules of gas to scatter sunlight from the **blue end** of the spectrum, there are really **not very many.** However, Mars's atmosphere **also** contains an **AWFUL LOT** of **DUST.** Dust particles **are much bigger** than **gas** molecules, which means that they scatter lots of sunlight from the **red end** of the spectrum.

Therefore, if you stood on the **surface** of Mars during the **daytime** and looked up at the **sky,** it would be mostly **red light** that ended up **reaching** your **eyes** – the opposite of what happens here on Earth. Wherever you **looked,** you'd see a **bright red sky!**

But, as **evening** approached and the Sun **dipped down** towards the **horizon**, its rays would have to travel a greater **distance** to reach your **eyes**. This means that the light from the **red end** of the spectrum would get scattered **SO MUCH** by the **thick Martian dust** that most of it would **bounce away** into **space**, leaving virtually **NONE** to reach your eyes **at all**. Only **light** from the blue end of the spectrum would make it to where you were standing, meaning you'd see ... a **bright blue sunset.** Cool or what?!

IF YOU LOOK **ONLINE** YOU CAN SEE EERIE PICTURES OF BLUE MARTIAN SUNSETS, AS CAPTURED BY THE ROBOTIC ROVERS CURIOSITY, SPIRIT AND OPPORTUNITY.

THE **ANSWER** IS **B**
ON MARS YOU MIGHT SEE A BLUE SUNSET.

Occasionally, a similarly **cool** thing can happen here on **Earth**. If a big **forest fire, drought** or **volcano** throws enough **dust** up into the sky, the dust particles will scatter most of the **red light** from the setting Sun away into **space**. Seeing as sunsets on Earth already **lack** light from the **blue end** of the spectrum, the **enormous** amounts of **dust** in the sky from a **rare** event like this can produce a **sunset** that is ... GREEN!

An event like this happened in 1883, when the **Krakatoa volcano** in Indonesia **erupted.** The explosion sent so much thick **dust and ash** into the sky that **green sunsets** were experienced across the world **FOR SEVERAL WEEKS!** Not only that, but the **scattering away** of **red light** by the **volcanic dust** made the light coming from the surface of the **Moon** appear **blue.** Some people say that this is where the expression **'once in a blue moon'** comes from – meaning something that **hardly ever happens.**

Although the phrase **blue moon** is also used to describe the occasions once every 2–3 years when you get a **second full moon** in the same month. Which is a bit **silly** really, as then the Moon isn't actually blue.

Whether **green, red** or **blue,** Mars and Earth are the **only places** in our solar system where colourful **sunsets** have been observed so far. However, scientists reckon that Titan, Saturn's largest moon, has a **dense enough atmosphere** that colourful sunsets could appear there too.

But I wouldn't suggest **going there** to find out. In many ways, Titan is remarkably **similar to Earth.** Not only does it have a **dense nitrogen-rich atmosphere,** but it's also the only other known place in the solar system that has a **cycle** in which liquids **rain down** from clouds, **flow** across its surface forming **lakes and seas,** and **evaporate** back into the sky — although on Titan this cycle involves **methane** rather than water, so you get **methane rain!** However, unlike our nice warm Earth, Titan's surface is a **blood-freezing -180°C.** Not to mention the fact that there's so little **oxygen** in the atmosphere that, without breathing apparatus, you'd **die.**

But did you know that you also might **die** if you **ate** one of these **strange-sounding** foods?

208

This list of **weird** body parts might sound pretty **terrifying** to even **contemplate** sinking your teeth into, but surprisingly, most of them are pretty **harmless.** And **some** of them are even quite **delicious.**

So what about eating a rattlesnake's tail? Surely **THAT** can't be a good idea?!

Well, you might be **surprised** to know that, in spite of their **deadly** nature, **rattlesnakes** (like all other snakes) are actually perfectly **safe to eat.** Some people even say they taste **quite yummy.** Apparently, cooked rattlesnake meat is **white** and **tender** and tastes like a cross between **frogs' legs** and **turtle.** Sounds ... er ... **slimy?**

Specials

C **A DUCK'S TESTICLES**

D **A TUNA FISH'S EYEBALL**

Now you might be thinking: but snakes can **poison** you! Surely eating one must be pretty dangerous? You'd think so, but, actually, no. You see, a snake can only **poison** you if its **venom** is injected **directly** into your **bloodstream.** That venom is stored in **glands** on the snake's **head** and is then squeezed into its **hollow fangs** when the snake **bites into** its prey. The venom is then injected through **little holes** in the sharp pointy ends of the fangs, straight into the prey's **bloodstream.** Ouch.

This means that, **IN THEORY,** as long as you **remove** a rattlesnake's **head,** there's **no chance** of getting any of its **poisonous venom.** Therefore, it is perfectly safe to eat the **rest of it.** Even the **tail**. (Although the **rattly** part wouldn't **taste** very good because it's made of **keratin,** which is the same hard substance that your **fingernails** are made of.)

I say 'in theory' because in **practice** it's not actually that **straightforward.** You see, it's pretty much **impossible** to actually **remove** the head of a venomous snake without risking being **bitten** and therefore poisoned. **EVEN IF IT'S ALREADY DEAD.**

WHAT??!
HOW CAN A SNAKE BiTE YOU iF iT'S DEAO??

Well, a snake has tiny **heat-sensitive pits** on either side of its head. When a **small rodent, lizard** or **unsuspecting human** happens to **approach** a live rattlesnake, the snake's heat-sensitive pits detect the **warmth** of the creature's body and this triggers a **bite-reflex.** Some snakes can detect the **faint body heat** of a creature as tiny as a **mouse** from up to **1 m away** and determine **EXACTLY** where it is.

The snake then attacks and **bites,** injecting **venom** into the bloodstream of its **prey,** which either **paralyses** it or **kills** it outright. The hungry snake then **swallows its prey whole!**

SNEAKY SNAKES MANAGE TO HUNT AT NIGHT BY USING THEIR HEAT-SENSITIVE PITS TO FOLLOW THE TRAIL OF HEAT LEFT BEHIND BY A MOVING ANIMAL.

If a **HUMAN** is unlucky enough to get **bitten** by a rattlesnake, the **nasty** venom causes **damage** to their skin tissues and blood cells, resulting in **pain, bruising** and **internal bleeding**. If the bite is left **untreated**, the damage can cause **severe problems** and can occasionally result in **death**. But, thankfully, if the person is able to get to a **hospital** in time and get an **antivenom** treatment **within 2 hours** of receiving the bite, there's a **99% chance** they'll **recover** just fine. Phew. (It's worth knowing that this isn't the case with **ALL** venomous snakes. For example, the bite of a **black mamba,** one of the **deadliest** snakes on the planet, can **kill** a human in **less than 30 minutes**. So your best bet is to **avoid** one of them.)

But here's the **crazy** part. The heat-sensitive pits on a snake's head remain **sensitive** to the warmth of an approaching creature for **several hours** after the snake is **DEAD**, which means that the **bite-reflex** can still be **triggered**. So a **DEAD SNAKE CAN BITE YOU**. But what's even **crazier** is that it can **still** bite you … **AFTER ITS HEAD HAS BEEN CUT OFF!**

To make matters worse, unlike **LIVING** snakes, **DEAD** snakes are not able to **regulate** the amount of **venom** they inject into their prey with their bite, so a bite from a **dead** snake might actually contain **EVEN MORE venom** than that of a **living** one. So, regardless of whether you fancy trying out **rattlesnake stew, PLEASE DO NOT APPROACH A RATTLESNAKE**. Even a dead one.

So, while it's **clear** that rattlesnakes can **kill** you, **eating** a rattlesnake's **tail** (that some other **foolish** person has prepared for you) **won't**.

WHAT ABOUT EATING A TUNA FISH'S EYEBALL? MIGHT THAT KILL YOU?

Actually, in countries such as China, Russia and Sri Lanka, **fish eyes** are considered a **delicacy**. Slimy eyeballs contain the **umami** flavour that many people really love. Umami is the **savoury** flavour that is normally associated with foods like **soy sauce, meat** and **seaweed**. Fish eyes are also surprisingly **nutritious,** as they contain high levels of **protein** and **omega 3 fatty acids,** which are good for your joints, your brain and your heart. In fact, in parts of southeast Asia, **the guest of honour** at a dinner party is usually served the **eyeballs** from a **whole steamed fish** or a **fish-head stew.** But in Japan, **tuna fish eyes** are simply sold off cheaply in **supermarkets.** After boiling or steaming, they're said to taste a little like **squid.**

SO WHAT ABOUT EATING TESTICLES? SURELY THEY CAN'T BE VERY TASTY?

Well, actually, **bulls' testicles** are the main ingredients of a commonly enjoyed Canadian dish called **Rocky Mountain Oysters,** sometimes known as **Prairie Oysters.** This bizarrely-named dish actually has nothing to do with **oysters** – it was just called that to make the idea of eating bulls' testicles sound a bit more **appealing.** The bull's **gigantic** (jacket-potato-sized) **rubbery** testicles are sliced, battered and fried and are said to taste a bit like **deer meat.**

Lambs' testicles, on the other hand, are the size of small **avocados** and have a strong **grassy** smell and an **OFFAL** taste that's apparently a bit like eating **stomach.** Mmm.

But as for a **duck's testicles** ... unbelievably, in some parts of the world they are quite a **delicacy.** They are about the size of **grapes** and are said to be both **delightfully tender** and **delicately flavoured. Who knew?!**

So that leaves a **polar bear's liver** as the thing from our list that's most likely to kill you if you ate it. Back in the 1500s, **Arctic explorers** found this out the **hard way ...**

You see, polar bears eat lots of **fish** and **seals,** and these creatures are rich in **vitamin A.** Vitamin A, also known as **retinol,** is important for **healthy growth** and **development.** The fact that seals have **high levels** of this useful vitamin in their fatty blubber allows them to easily **nourish** their **babies** in a harsh and cold environment.

Vitamin A also helps the body's **immune system** to fight against **illness** and **infection** and is needed for **good vision** – to help animals see well when the **light is low.**

Small amounts of vitamin A are present in **eggs, cheese** and lots of **fruits and vegetables.** But there's **quite a bit** in kale, broccoli

leaves, butter, sweet potatoes and carrots – hence why people sometimes say that **eating carrots** can help you **see in the dark.** Although this isn't **QUITE** true. While the vitamin A in carrots will ensure that you retain your **natural ability** to see well in **low light conditions,** it sadly won't allow you to see in **total darkness.** No matter how many of the **pointy orange** things you manage to consume.

OK, so what has all this got to do with a **polar bear's liver?** Well, here's the thing. Vitamin A is a **fat-soluble** vitamin. This means that, unlike **other** vitamins, it does not **dissolve** in **water.** Which means that, once the vitamin has been **eaten,** excess amounts can't be **lost** from the body in watery **wee.** Instead, it accumulates in the animal's **liver.**

As a result, pretty much all animals contain **quite high levels** of vitamin A in their **livers.** In fact, humans can get **LOADS** of vitamin A from eating **cod liver oil** or the **livers** of animals such as turkeys, chickens, cows, pigs or fish.

Now, because polar bears eat **SO MUCH** vitamin A-rich fish and seals, they end up with an **AWFUL LOT** of vitamin A in their livers. Luckily this works out fine for them because their livers have **evolved** to be able to **tolerate** super-high levels of this vitamin.

However, humans and other animals are not so **lucky.** Their livers would simply not be able to **cope** with such high levels. Which means that if a human happened to take in **too much** vitamin A, say, by ... I don't know ... eating a polar bear's liver, the vitamin A in **THEIR** liver could accumulate to **POISONOUS** levels. This would result in a **nasty condition** known as **Hypervitaminosis A,** which can cause drowsiness, vomiting, blurred vision, headaches, bone pain and even **death.**

And this is **exactly** what happened to some poor unsuspecting **Arctic explorers.** They'd become so **hungry** that they were **forced** to munch on some **juicy polar bear meat** ... including its **vitamin A-packed** liver. And sadly some of them didn't live to tell the tale.

So, if **YOU** were to eat a polar bear's liver (not that you'd be likely to **stumble across one** in your local supermarket), there's a good chance that it could kill you. So please **don't** do that.

THE **ANSWER** is **B** YOU MIGHT DIE IF YOU ATE A POLAR BEAR'S LIVER.

You probably know that, today, it's not explorers but **polar bears THEMSELVES** that are going **hungry** in the Arctic. Many creatures who live in the Arctic depend on **freezing cold ice.** So, as **temperatures rise** and **ice melts** due to **global warming,** we are seeing **big impacts** on creatures in that region. Sadly, it's some of the animals we **love the most** that are suffering.

Polar bears need to stand on floating **sea ice** when they're out hunting for **seals** in the freezing Northern seas. However, this **sea ice** is rapidly **melting.** This means that poor old polar bears are now forced to **walk** or **swim ENORMOUS distances** to get to any remaining ice. Or they have to make do with foraging for food on **land** where there is far less **prey.**

In fact, some polar bears are getting **so hungry** that they have resorted to **scavenging** for food where **humans** live. In February 2019, a terrifying troupe of **50 polar bears** invaded the remote Russian town of Belushya Guba in search of food. Videos posted on social media showed the **scrawny starving creatures** picking their way through **rubbish bins,** rummaging through **dumps** and even roaming around inside **buildings.** Poor old polar bears.

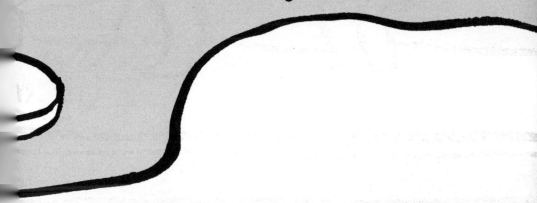

SO WHY IS SO MUCH SEA ICE MELTING?

Well, as you know, the Earth is heating up. But what you might **NOT** know is that **global warming** is causing the Arctic (and part of the Antarctic) to warm up more than **twice as fast** as the average for the planet. And warmer **air** not only melts sea ice from **above**, but warmer **oceans** melt sea ice from **below**. Double whammy.

To add to this, while the **bright white surface** of ice **reflects** a lot of the Sun's heat back from its surface, once the ice **melts** it **exposes** the **darker surface** of the water below it. This darker ocean surface can **absorb** more of the heat from the Sun (kinda like how wearing a **black T-shirt** on a sunny day makes you feel **hotter** than wearing a **white one**). The **extra heat** absorbed by the ocean then melts **even more** ice, exposing **even more** dark water, which causes **even more** ice to melt ... and so on and so on. This worrying **feedback loop** is increasing the amount of **sea ice** that is **melting** as a result of global warming.

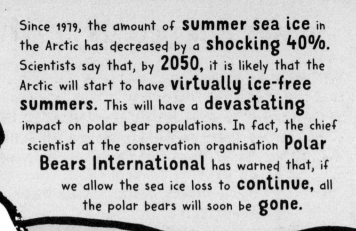

Since 1979, the amount of **summer sea ice** in the Arctic has decreased by a **shocking 40%**. Scientists say that, by **2050**, it is likely that the Arctic will start to have **virtually ice-free summers**. This will have a **devastating** impact on polar bear populations. In fact, the chief scientist at the conservation organisation **Polar Bears International** has warned that, if we allow the sea ice loss to **continue**, all the polar bears will soon be **gone**.

What's **really sad** about the effects of global warming on **sea ice** is that we don't have a way of **reversing the damage** and getting the sea ice that we've already lost **back**. That's why it's so **important** that us humans stop putting **even more greenhouse gases** into the atmosphere, so that we can try to prevent **EVEN MORE** warming that could cause further changes to our planet.

As I mentioned earlier, one of the effects of **global warming** is **rising sea levels** due to melting ice. But the good news is that when **sea ice** melts, it **doesn't actually affect sea levels.** Phew.

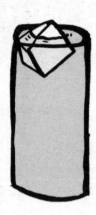

If you don't **believe** me, try putting an **ice cube** in a glass of **water** and then **fill** the glass right to the **brim**, so that the top of the ice cube **pokes up over** the top of the glass. Leave it for a while so the ice **melts**. When you come **back**, you might be **surprised** to find that the water **hasn't spilled over** the edge of the glass. **MAGIC!**

Why is this? Well, ice is **less dense** than water, so the water that the ice cube **turns into** takes up **less space** than the ice did – so now the **pokey-up bit** fits into the glass too. This is exactly what happens when **sea ice** melts.

So **melting ice** is no problem unless you're a **polar bear,** right? Not quite ...
You see, it's not just **sea ice** that's melting due to **global warming.** So too is ice on **LAND.** And the **problem** is, when land-based **ice melts**, all the **water** that was held in the ice now runs off into the **oceans** ...

... and this **DOES** cause sea levels to **rise.** Just like what would happen if you put **more water** into your glass.

Greenland, the second largest ice sheet in the world, is now losing ice **7 times faster** per year than it was in the 1990s. The icy continent of **Antarctica** (the world's **largest** ice sheet, found at the **South Pole**) has lost **3 trillion tonnes** of ice in the past 25 years.

Glaciers are also losing their ice rapidly, such as those in **icy mountain ranges** like the Himalayas, the Andes and the Alps. This is of huge **concern**, as nearly **2 billion people** depend on **fresh water** from mountain glaciers like these. It's predicted that **the Alps** could become almost completely **ice-free** by the end of the century.

The total amount of ice that's been lost from our planet due to global warming over the past 40 years is the equivalent of losing 300 chunks of ice, each one the size of a double-decker bus, **EVERY SECOND.**

Not only is there **more water in the oceans** from the melting of ice sheets and glaciers, but as the ocean water gets warmer due to rising temperatures, the water **expands** and takes up **more space.** And this causes sea levels to **rise even further.**

Rising sea levels are already having a **huge impact** on **coastal communities** around the world. Experts say that we need to make some **serious changes** or, by **2050,** rising seas will be likely to **flood the land** where more than **300 million people** currently live – **at least once a year.** Large parts of **Vietnam** and other **low-lying countries** could practically **disappear.** The **UK** will be one of the countries **severely** affected, with large parts of the **English coastline** and areas around its **rivers** predicted to regularly fall **below sea level** by the year 2050.

By the **end of the century** we could see sea levels rise by **1 m** or more, potentially leaving the homes of **230 million people** below the **waterline** at **high tide,** meaning they could experience **flooding** on a **daily basis.** To make matters worse, if the West Antarctic Ice Sheet **collapses,** and it looks like it may well do, that could mean sea levels would rise by **several metres** in the coming centuries, which would be **absolutely catastrophic.**

GOSH iT'S DYiNG!

The **best thing** we can do is to make sure we stop **adding more greenhouse gases** to our **fluffy blanket** as soon as possible. We can also **make plans** that mean the people all over the world who could be made **homeless** by rising water have **somewhere new and safe to live.**

In terms of wildlife, it's not just our **beloved polar bears** that are **suffering** as a result of **melting ice** and **warmer oceans.** A whopping **90%** of the **increased heat** trapped in our atmosphere is being **STORED** in the oceans, and this is having a **devastating** effect on some of the **creatures** that live within them. **Indeed, marine heatwaves** are already **killing** huge numbers of **sea creatures** and destroying **crucial species,** such as **seagrass** and **kelp,** that provide **shelter** and **food** to many other ocean creatures.

Some are creatures that we **eat,** some are ones we **love to look at** and **learn about** and some are creatures that we **never really see** and may not even **know about** but are part of **ocean ecosystems** that we all **depend on.** In fact, there are around **3 billion** people across the globe who **rely on seafood** as their main source of **protein.**

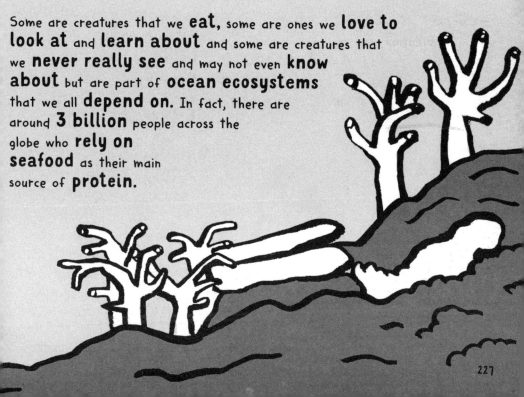

Ocean heating has also caused the death of nearly **half** of the world's **coral**. Tropical **coral reefs** are not only some of the most **beautiful** ecosystems on the face of the Earth, but they are also some of the most **important** and **diverse** ones too, supporting up to **1 million** other species and providing **food**, livelihoods, **tourism** and **storm protection** for **half a billion people** across the globe. It is predicted that, within the next **10 years**, a devastating **70–90%** of our tropical coral reefs will have been **lost.** Unless we take **rapid action**, by **2050** they will have been virtually **wiped out.**

Ocean heating not only damages sea life **directly**, but also causes the **oxygen** that is usually **dissolved** in seawater to become less **soluble.** This can result in areas of water with **extremely low** levels of oxygen. Such areas are known as **ocean dead zones** because the **lack of oxygen** can cause **sea creatures** living within them to **suffocate.** Plus, some of the extra **carbon dioxide** that's in our atmosphere is being **absorbed** by the oceans, making the water **more acidic.** Increasing ocean acidity is already **dissolving the shells** of some small creatures, such as oysters, clams and sea snails.

Whilst the **saddest thing** about **melting ice** is that it **cannot be reversed** – meaning we can't **make things better** for all those **hungry polar bears** – it **may be possible** to help our ocean waters to **cool down,** which would be **great news** for many sea creatures. More on this in a bit.

While **some ocean recovery** may indeed be possible, all the terrible impacts of **excess carbon dioxide, warming oceans** and **melting ice** that I've talked about in this chapter are further **reminders** as to why we must now all **work together** to try to **reduce greenhouse gas emissions** as soon as possible, so we can stop our planet from getting any **hotter** +!

it already is.
But don't **worry,** in the **final section** of this book (coming up next) I'll remind you of all the things that **YOU** and your **family** can do to help. And I'll share with you a few **inspiring** stories of **projects** that are already going on. Projects that bring **hope** to the world – and to all the **creatures** who live on it.

SO WHAT CAN YOU DO TO HELP THE PLANET?

Thank you for **reading** this book. In it I wanted to **share** with you some of the things about the Earth that I find the most **fascinating,** but also those that make me feel the most **sad.**

While you've been **reading** this book there might have been times when **you** felt **sad** too, or **scared** or **angry** about what is happening on our planet. Perhaps you felt **anxious.** Or **overwhelmed.** Maybe you felt kinda **numb.** Or a bit **confused.** You may have felt **frustrated** that some people around you don't really seem to **understand** or **care** what's happening. Or maybe you felt absolutely **nothing** at all.

Don't worry, **ALL** of these feelings are perfectly **normal,** and I can promise you that you're **not alone.**

Sometimes I feel **scared** or **sad** too. Some days I want to **cry** about it. Some days I feel **frustrated** that people don't seem to be **listening.** Some days I feel **angry** that the people **in charge** aren't doing nearly enough to **make things better.** Sometimes I just feel like it's all a bit too much and I want to stay in bed and watch **Netflix** and eat **ice cream.** So I do. But then I **read** about some of the **amazing projects** and **awesome new research** that's going on out there, and I'm **inspired** by the **hope** of a brighter, kinder, and more beautiful **future.** And then, when I feel **better,** I focus on the things that I **CAN** do to help.

So, I wanted to finish this book by **reminding** you of some of the small things I've already mentioned throughout this book that **YOU** and your **family** can do to make a **difference** to our planet, and to offer you a few **other ideas** and **hopeful stories** too.

1. THINK ABOUT HOW YOU SHOP – REMEMBER THE FOUR 'R'S: REDUCE, REUSE, REPAIR, RECYCLE

It's a really good idea to try to **buy less stuff.** It can be **fun** to **repair** what you already have or to find **new uses** for old toys or clothes instead – we call this **upcycling.** And if you decide to get rid of some old things, try to **recycle** them by giving them to a friend or a **charity shop.** (Although remember, when it comes to **plastic,** it's far better to just **buy less** in the first place.) If you do need to **buy** something, buying **second-hand** is much **better** for the planet. But if what you need does have to be bought **NEW,** try to avoid '**fast fashion**' and buying on **impulse,** and instead **take your time** and choose things that are **made to last** – as they won't need **replacing** as often. And finally, look out for things that have been **made locally.**

2. THINK ABOUT WHAT YOU EAT

If you haven't already, try to **cut down** on the amount of **animal products** that you eat and drink – especially **beef, lamb** and **cows' milk.** Sadly that includes all products **made from** cow's milk, such as **cheese, butter** and **yoghurt.** There are lots of yummy **vegan cheeses** out there you can try instead though. You can even get **vegan pizzas!**

Ask your parents to look out for **fruit and veggies** that have been grown **organically** and **sustainably.** These do often cost a bit more **money** though, so don't worry if this solution is **hard** for you. Also, try to encourage your family to buy fruit and vegetables that have been grown **locally** and '**in season**'. Some local farmers grow vegetables '**out of season**' (at a time when they wouldn't naturally grow), which requires **heated greenhouses** that release **greenhouse gases** – defeating the point of buying **locally**.

It's worth knowing that British **blackberries, raspberries, strawberries** and **tomatoes** are in season throughout the **summer** and **autumn** months. British **potatoes** are in season in the autumn, so **stock up** on those then, and British **apples** are in season during the chilly **winter** months – perfect timing for a nice warm **apple crumble. Yum.** British **carrots,** on the other hand, are in season pretty much **all year round.** No excuses there then.

veggie burger

HURRAY FOR CARROTS!

And do take pity on **weird and knobbly** fruits and vegetables that no one else wants to buy. Even better, if you can, **grow your own!**

It's also a good idea to try to only buy **as much food** as you know your family can **get through** before it goes **bad,** so less gets wasted.

3. THINK ABOUT HOW YOU TRAVEL

Obviously going on holidays **abroad** is exciting – but don't forget that taking **trains** or **buses** can be a **fun alternative** to **aeroplanes**, and are a good way to **see** the country. If you can't **avoid** flying, some **airlines** say they will **make up for** the carbon emissions of your flight by doing things to **look after** the planet, like **planting trees.** These are called 'carbon offsetting' schemes. But do make sure you choose one that has the 'Gold Standard' logo, as sadly most of the rest **don't actually work.**

> A STAGGERING 9 OUT OF 10 PEOPLE ON OUR PLANET BREATHE POLLUTED AIR.

Walk or **cycle** to school if you can, and try to encourage your family to travel by **car** as **little** as possible. You see, traditional cars have **internal combustion engines** that burn **petrol** or **diesel**, which are **fossil fuels.**

You might have heard people talking about getting an **electric car** to replace their old one. Electric cars are certainly not **perfect,** but they are a **lot better** than traditional cars. You still have to take into account the **carbon emissions** that come from the **manufacturing** of an electric car – and from generating the **electricity** that will be needed to make it **run** –

but even so, an **electric car** currently releases less than **one-third as much** carbon dioxide as a conventional car over its lifetime. And soon this could be **even less** as we start to generate more and more **electricity** using **renewable energy.**

Plus, electric cars reduce **air pollution** by about **45%.**

Whilst electric cars are certainly a big **improvement,** cutting back on using the car as much as you can is a **far better** idea. Taking an **electric bus** might soon be a good alternative, as a lot more people can **fit into** a bus than a car. In fact, it is predicted that by 2025, **half** of the world's buses will be electric.

4. GO GREEN AT HOME

You could talk to your **family** and find out if they would consider switching to a **green energy provider** for your home's electricity. Today there are lots of **energy companies** that provide **100% renewable energy** at little or no extra **cost**. Who knows, maybe you already are using one of them?! The best ones will get their energy **directly** from **renewable sources,** such as **wind** or **solar power.** Perhaps you could **help your parents** find out about **what options** are available where you **live.** You could also ask your family to **check** that your home is **well insulated** so less of the energy you use **heating** your home **escapes** into the atmosphere and gets **wasted.** That'll save them **money** too.

> SPEAKING OF WHICH ...

5. INVEST MONEY WISELY

Here's a tip you could share with your **parents** that they might not know about. Across the world, there are **35 banks** that have invested a horrifying **£2.2 trillion** in the **fossil fuel industry** since 2016, including some of the **big banks** in the UK. You probably don't want any money your parents may be carefully **putting aside** into their **bank accounts** being used to help **burn more fossil fuels.** So it's a really good idea to check your family is **aware** of what's happening to any of their **money,** and to try and **avoid** banks that do this.

6. PLANT TREES

So far, all the ways I've suggested for how you can **help** have been about trying to **limit** how much **FURTHER DAMAGE** is done to our planet, by **cutting down** on things that are increasing **greenhouse gas emissions** (as well as damaging our **soils** and destroying our **trees** and **wildlife**).

But we can also help by **looking after** and **restoring** our planet's **NATURAL** methods of **removing** carbon dioxide from our atmosphere. One of the most powerful ways we can do this is by **planting more trees.** And that's something **YOU** can do to help. Have a look at the websites for **environmental charities,** such as **The Woodland Trust,** to see how you can get involved.

However, it's important to be aware that **planting trees** must be done **as well as**, not **instead of**, the other **changes** I've already spoken about. Some people think if we **plant enough trees** we can **carry on** burning fossil fuels. But that's simply not true. If we want to **offset** all the **greenhouse gases** we're releasing, we'd need to plant at least **10 million square km** of new forest. That's an area of forest the size of the entire **United States of America**, consisting of a **staggering 1 trillion trees**. I think we can safely agree that's a virtually **impossible** task.

However, every single **extra tree** does help. Every **fraction of a degree** by which we are able to **limit** global warming really will make a **difference**. There are nearly **8 billion people** on our planet – imagine what an **impact** it would have if everyone planted **just one tree** ...

7. GET INVOLVED IN REWILDING PROJECTS TO RESTORE NATURAL WILDLIFE

Another great way you can help is by getting involved in exciting **REWILDING** projects that aim to **restore the damage** that's already been done to our planet – by **bringing back** natural wildlife. This can be through **mass reforestation, repairing** damaged land, **reclaiming** animals' natural habitats or **reintroducing** animals to their natural homes. Many such projects are **already** taking place all over the world. There may even be some **near you** that you can go and **visit.** Here are a few of my **favourite** examples:

One exciting **rewilding** project is taking place in **mid-Wales** where in recent years there had been a terrible **decline** in the numbers of **pine martens** (a sort of cat-sized weasel). This was due to large areas of **woodland** being **cleared** and **gamekeepers** taking control of the populations of **predators,** such as pine martens. The Vincent Wildlife Pine Marten Recovery Project are now in the process of bringing new pine martens down from **Scotland** and releasing them into **20 woodland sites** across mid-Wales, **restoring** the cute creatures to their **native habitats.**

Speaking of **Scotland**, about 20 years ago, a group of friends bought a beautiful **650 hectares valley** in the Moffat Hills. Their aim was to **restore** a huge area of **wild woodland** to how it would have looked around **6,000 years ago.** Their project, known as the Carrifran Wildwood Project has now seen the planting of over **600,000 native trees.** Native trees are better than trees from **overseas** because they help support **wildlife** as well as the climate.

And in **England,** when **new owners** took over the Knepp Castle Estate a few decades ago, they were **horrified** to find that it had been **ploughed** and **farmed** so **intensively** that there was virtually no **wildlife** left. So they replaced the **dairy cows** with a diverse array of **more natural** grazing animals, such as Old English Longhorn cattle, Exmoor ponies, Tamworth pigs and deer, which allowed lots of **new plants** to grow. Since then, there has been an **extraordinary** increase in wildlife. Even some **extremely rare** species – such as **turtle doves** and **purple emperor butterflies** – are now **breeding** there.

Even if you live in a **big city,** you can get involved in exciting **urban rewilding projects,** such as **restoring** neglected wild habitats, cleaning up **waterways,** creating **city butterfly meadows,** building **unlikely homes** for birds of prey, or even just **collecting litter** in green spaces. Sometimes **small changes** are all it takes to tempt **species** to come and live in a **busy city.** Indeed, **freshwater insects** have already been increasing by about **11% per decade,** probably as a result of recent attempts to **clean up** our waters.

What's even more exciting (and incredibly reassuring) is that, when nature is **left to do its own thing,** sometimes it can recover **all by itself** – without needing any **human help AT ALL.**

A great example of this is happening in the Netherlands, beside the River Rhine, on some land that used to be **dairy and maize farms.** At the time of the farms, there were **no trees** growing on the land, **no plants** in the river and virtually **no other wildlife.** However, about 25 years ago, the Dutch government **bought** the farmland and **closed down** all the farms. The idea was that the River Rhine could **flow into** this land when it **flooded,** therefore **protecting** cities downstream. For decades, the land was left **alone.** Since then, there has been an **explosion** in wildlife. Beavers, eagles, butterflies and even wolves have been **returning** to the area.

Not only that, but **ecotourism** is now bringing **visitors** to the area, increasing the **local economy**. At least **5 times** as many **jobs** have been **created** as were **lost** when the farms closed down.

It's even possible to **restore wildlife** in our **OCEANS** too. 'Marine permaculture' projects are currently underway in the South Pacific, which involve **growing seaweed** on giant underwater structures. **Cool water** and **nutrients** are brought up from deep in the ocean by a **pump** that's powered by the natural rise and fall of the sea, **cooling** the water near the surface and providing **food** for the **seaweed**. The seaweed provides new **habitats** for **fish** – restoring **ocean life** – and also **traps carbon** from the atmosphere as it grows. Small-scale projects like this have already seen huge improvements in **water quality** and a return of **marine life**. If, in the future, we can **scale them up,** the possibilities will be **endless**. Excess seaweed could even be used as **food** for humans, **fertiliser** for land crops or **biofuels** to provide **clean energy**.

Stories like these offer **hope** to our world.

8. UNDERSTAND ABOUT RENEWABLE AND CLEANER ENERGY

Although fossil fuels are clearly not the **way forward,** we do still need **energy.** But what's **great** is that there are now many **cleaner alternatives** for meeting our planet's ever-increasing **energy demands** that don't add **greenhouse gases** to our atmosphere. These include **solar, wind, waves, nuclear** and **geothermal** (heat energy from deep within the Earth). If you **understand** how important **clean energy** is, then you will be able to tell **other people** about it so they can understand too - **YOU** can help **spread the word!**

Wind energy is so **easy to come by** that it could supply the **entire world's** energy needs **40 times over.** Plus, wind farms can be built **'offshore',** meaning they don't take up **any land.** Wind energy is now the **cheapest** energy to **produce** in the UK. By 2030, Britain plans to generate **one-third** of its power from wind.

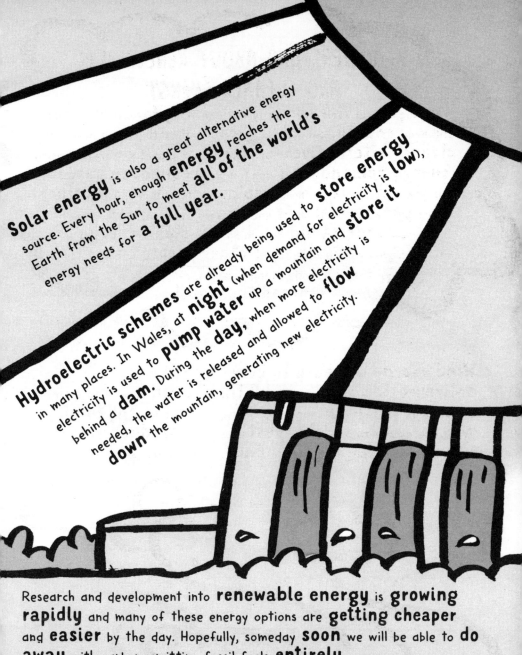

Solar energy is also a great alternative energy source. Every hour, enough **energy** reaches the Earth from the Sun to meet **all of the world's** energy needs for **a full year.**

Hydroelectric schemes are already being used to **store energy** in many places. In Wales, at **night** (when demand for electricity is **low**), electricity is used to **pump water** up a mountain and **store it** behind a **dam.** During the **day,** when more electricity is needed, the water is released and allowed to **flow down** the mountain, generating new electricity.

Research and development into **renewable energy** is **growing rapidly** and many of these energy options are **getting cheaper** and **easier** by the day. Hopefully, someday **soon** we will be able to **do away** with carbon-emitting fossil fuels **entirely.**

9. YOU DON'T HAVE TO DO IT ALL ON YOUR OWN...

There have been a **great many** things I've suggested in this chapter that you can personally do to help **protect** the planet. However, it's also important to **remember** that you don't have to do it **ALL**. In fact, you absolutely **CAN'T** do this on your own.

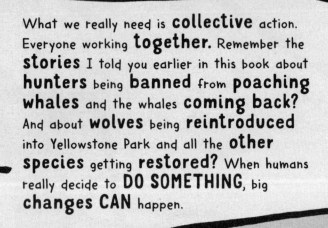

What we really need is **collective** action. Everyone working **together.** Remember the **stories** I told you earlier in this book about **hunters** being **banned** from **poaching whales** and the whales **coming back?** And about **wolves** being **reintroduced** into Yellowstone Park and all the **other species** getting **restored?** When humans really decide to **DO SOMETHING**, big **changes CAN** happen.

Here's **one final story** about how humans around the world listened to **warnings from scientists** and **came together** to make a **big change.**

In the early 1980s, scientists discovered that there was a hole in something called the **ozone layer.** You might know that the ozone layer acts like a sort of **sunshade** around our planet, **protecting** us from most of the **harmful UV rays** from the Sun. Scientists had found that this **worrying** hole was linked to our use of **chemicals** called **CFCs.**

Luckily, many world leaders **recognised** how **dangerous** the situation was. In 1989, they signed an agreement that said we needed to **limit** the use of **CFC chemicals,** such as **aerosol sprays,** across the globe. Disaster was **averted.** Thankfully, the hole in the ozone layer is now **shrinking** and it is predicted that, eventually, it will **heal entirely.** Good work humans!

The point is, when humans and governments really **try,** we really **CAN** make things better. And it's not **too late** for us to make a **REAL DIFFERENCE** with climate change and wildlife loss too.

10. REMEMBER YOU CAN MAKE A DiFFERENCE

To fix this mess we all need to **work together.** Governments, adults and children. But the good news is that if we **each** just do our own **little bit,** together we **can** make an **ENORMOUS** difference.

You're **never too small** to have an impact. Look at **Greta Thunberg.** She carried out her first **'School Strike for Climate'** at the age of **15,** sitting alone in front of the **Swedish Parliament** building holding a **placard.** At first, everyone **ignored** her. But she **stuck with it** and within 4 months she had become **recognised** across the globe and was invited to speak at the **United Nations Climate Talks** in Poland where she **criticised** world leaders for **failing to do enough** to address **climate change.** By the age of 16, she had started an **international youth movement** – the 'Fridays for Future' school strikes. Within **a year** she had inspired more than **7 million people** across the globe to join her, had **written a book** about her experiences and had won the **International Children's Peace Prize.**

So, whether it's starting an **eco-council** at school, asking to meet your **local MP** or **city councillors** (with your parents or teachers), joining a group such as **Greenpeace** or **The Woodland Trust**, campaigning for a **better world**, changing the way you **eat**, the stuff you **buy** or the way you **travel**, or **helping** to **educate** your parents, siblings or friends about what's going on on our planet (and how **THEY** can help), there's always **SOMETHING** you can do.

Maybe you might even **get involved** with some of the inspiring projects I've talked about in this book. Or perhaps you might **become a scientist** or an **engineer** yourself and come up with some **other** exciting ways to **help** the planet.

So, where does this **leave** us? Well, my **final** piece of advice is to **appreciate** – and try to be **happy** with – what you **already have**.

Spend time doing things you **love.** Whether that's a **walk** in **nature** with your family or your dog, **reading a book** quietly on your own or **getting up to mischief** with your friends. Perhaps you'll discover that you don't need **far-flung holidays** or more and more **trendy clothes** or **computer games** to be **truly happy** after all.

And the **MOST** important thing that we can do is to be **kind** to each other. And to all the other **creatures** living on this planet. Let's **work together** to make the world a better place. For us, and for all the **beautiful beings,** large and small, that we share it with.

WRITE YOUR OWN QUESTIONS HERE

_____

_____

_____

_____

_____

_____

_____

_____

WRITE YOUR **OWN** QUESTIONS HERE

Acknowledgements

I'd like to thank these brilliant scientists for helping make sure all the facts in this book are correct and up to date:

Dr Scott Archer-Nicholls, Atmospheric Scientist at the University of Cambridge; Professor Richard Betts MBE, Head of Climate Impacts Research at the Met Office Hadley Centre and Chair in Climate Impacts at the University of Exeter; Professor James Bullock, Conservation Ecologist at the UK Centre for Ecology and Hydrology; Dr Tamsin Edwards, Climate Scientist at King's College London; Dr Alex Farnsworth, Climate Scientist at the University of Bristol; Professor Helen Amanda Fricker, Glaciologist at the Scripps Polar Centre; Dr Charlie Gardner, Conservation Scientist at the University of Kent; Professor Ed Hawkins, Climate Scientist at the University of Reading; Dr Wolfgang Knorr, Earth System Scientist at Lund University; Professor Mark Maslin, Earth System Scientist at University College London; Professor Rich Pancost, Head of the School of Earth Sciences at the University of Bristol; Dr Glen Peters, Research Director at the CICERO Centre for International Climate Research; Professor Andy Purvis, Biodiversity Researcher at The Natural History Museum; Professor Julia Steinberger, Social Ecologist at the University of Lausanne; Dr Aaron Thierry, Ecologist and Climate Communicator; Dr Charlie JR Williams, Climate Scientist at the Universities of Bristol and Reading.

And thank you to Andy Wynne, Educational Psychologist and director of Healthy Mind UK*, for helping me communicate the facts in a way that wasn't too scary.

I'd also like to thank my brilliant publisher Isobel for getting on board with this book and being so supportive, my amazing dad for reading every word and making sure it all made sense, and my wonderful partner Kimwei for believing in this book and being with me every step of the way. I couldn't have done it without you.

*Healthy Mind UK delivers innovative 'Ecoheadz' primary school projects across the UK with an aim to educate children about climate change and how it affects our mental health